Postal Propaganda of the Third Reich

Albert L. Moore

Schiffer Military History
Atglen, PA

Dedication
This book is lovingly dedicated to Diane, Wesley and Lisa. Without their love,
help, and tolerance, this book would not have been possible.

"Be watchful, stand firm in your
faith, be courageous, be strong.
Let all that you do be done in love."
– 1 Corinthians 16:13-14

On the front cover:
Official German postcard for "Stamp Day," 1942. Artwork by Ax-Heu. Author's Collection.

Book design by Robert Biondi.

Copyright © 2003 by Albert L. Moore.
Library of Congress Catalog Number: 2003102927.

Printed in China.
ISBN: 0-7643-1867-5

We are always looking for people to write books on new and related subjects. If you have an idea for a book, please contact us at the address below.

Published by Schiffer Publishing Ltd.
4880 Lower Valley Road
Atglen, PA 19310
Phone: (610) 593-1777
FAX: (610) 593-2002
E-mail: Info@schifferbooks.com.
Visit our web site at: www.schifferbooks.com
Please write for a free catalog.
This book may be purchased from the publisher.
Please include $3.95 postage.
Try your bookstore first.

In Europe, Schiffer books are distributed by:
Bushwood Books
6 Marksbury Ave.
Kew Gardens
Surrey TW9 4JF
England
Phone: 44 (0)20 8392-8585
FAX: 44 (0)20 8392-9876
E-mail: Bushwd@aol.com.
Free postage in the UK. Europe: air mail at cost.
Try your bookstore first.

Contents

Acknowledgments

A s the author of this book, I can honestly say that it would not have been possible without the help of several other people. First of all, I would like to acknowledge the help of the faculty and staff of California State University at Dominguez Hills, especially Dr. Howard Holter, who encouraged me to seek publication of my Master's Thesis. Next, I would like to thank Hugh Chambers for his outstanding work photographing the numerous postal items and related materials included in this project. I would also like to thank my editor at Schiffer, Bob Biondi, for his expert guidance in the tedious process of transforming a thesis into a book. Many thanks also go out to Roger Bender and Ann Vachon for their kindness in allowing me to reprint illustrations from their fascinating books! Another significant person I would like to recognize is Dr. Frank Lojewski, one of my undergraduate professors at Indiana University at Kokomo. He provided fascinating History lectures making the subjects come alive for me. His masterful teaching transformed my interest in History into a life long love and fascination. I am certain that I would not have written this book without his inspiration. Finally, I would like to express my appreciation to my family for their support and assistance in helping me write this book. I truly appreciate the patience and understanding of my children, Wesley and Lisa. Not only did they have to endure many dinner conversations centering on postal propaganda (not too interesting to most teenagers), they also got booted off of the family computer several evenings so that the author could work a few more hours on this book. And, last but not least, I would like to thank my wife, Diane. I am truly grateful for her loving and arduous work assisting me with so much of the typing and editing necessary in this project. Thank you for your love, encouragement, and exhaustive work on this project and for all that you do every single day!

Introduction

For me, the study of history has always been fascinating. I believe this is due, in part, to my belief that one can best approach historical subjects by seeking to imagine one's self actually experiencing the events first hand. In some historical settings this can be quite difficult because of the chronological or cultural remoteness of the particular period in question.

This is the case for many people with regard to the study of the Third Reich in Germany. Perhaps, in part, because of our nation's entry into the war against Germany, the Third Reich is looked upon in terms of absolutes. It is seen as an unabashedly evil nation whose people committed unspeakable crimes and atrocities and which deservedly lost the war. For many, therefore, there is little need to delve much deeper into the subject.

But in many respects, the Germany of the 1930s and 1940s was a nation not greatly unlike our own. She was an industrialized nation with a similar mix of rural and urban citizens. Furthermore, as an European nation, Germany shared many of the same cultural, artistic and religious characteristics prevalent in the United States at that time. And, while the United States may not have shared the anti-Semitic obsession that large segments of the German population possessed, one could certainly observe much evidence of racism and anti-Semitism in our own country. There may not have been as many overt signs of these prejudices, but there were countless subtle examples. For instance, my own father recalled that in the late 1930s or early 1940s he visited a public park in a small town in Central

Illinois. Upon entering the grounds, he was confronted with a sign containing the words: "No Dogs or Jews."

Perhaps the greatest difference between Germany and the United States during this era was the fact that American "nativism" and racism never succeeded in finding a broad-based and successful political voice in the way it did in Germany and a few other European nations. Additionally, few, if any, inside Germany at the time (even among the Jews) would have looked upon their nation as intrinsically evil. That view, when it did exist, was generally reserved for those looking at Germany from the outside. For the German people, this place was simply home. A chilling memory of an imprisoned anti-Nazi woman acknowledges this German mind set:

> Let me try to tell you what that time was like in Germany: I was sitting in a cinema with a Jewish friend and her daughter of thirteen, while a Nazi parade went across the screen, and the girl caught her mother's arm and whispered, 'Oh, Mother, Mother, if I weren't a Jew, I think I'd be a Nazi!' No one outside seems to understand how this was.[1]

Ironically, most Jews even found it a home still worth remaining a part of well after Hitler and his party assumed control.

In this book, I will look "up close" at German life and explore how attitudes and perceptions were shaped and perhaps changed during World War Two. To gain this "up close" look at German life, I will examine one of the most ordinary and mundane aspects of any modern society: its postal materials. I hope to show the enormous significance of postal related materials when used as a tool by the Nazi regime to gain support for its ideas and subsequent rise to power. Through an exploration of this medium, I believe one can better imagine what life must have been like for citizens in Germany. By examining the documents and material that Germans found regularly within their very own mailboxes, we will come closer to understanding the overwhelming psychological and political pressures which every German must have experienced. Whether a staunch supporter looking for validation or a brooding opponent expecting the worst, the postal materials of Nazi Germany can help us better understand the power of the messages that every German received daily and even consider what our own response might have been to a "steady diet" of such subtle, repetitive propaganda.

I believe that this book will provide a valuable method of examining the Third Reich that is both illuminating and unique. There are numerous excellent works of social history on the subject, such as *Hitler's Social Revolution* by David Schoenbaum and *The Twelve Year Reich* by Richard Grunberger, that help us understand many facets of the day to day experiences of "ordinary" Germans. Other books, such as Christopher R. Browning's *Ordinary Men* or *Hitler's Willing Executioners* by Daniel Jonah Goldhagen, even delve into the question of how and why everyday Germans participated in some of the regime's most criminal acts. There are even a few works on the subject of postal material that focus on the "mechanics" of this subject. Books like *Postcards of Hitler's Germany* by R. James Bender and *I'll Be Seeing You* by Tonie and Valmai Holt are helpful in illustrating and cataloging some of the postal materials. And, while there are many works about propaganda in general, exploration of the form and impact of postal propaganda within the Third Reich has been largely absent.

In the pages that follow, I have sought to study the social fabric of Nazi Germany through an examination of Germany's postal material. I believe that this unique approach will help to shed new light upon our study of German history. My analysis of the postcards, postmarks, stamps and mail of the Third Reich will reveal some of the realities of everyday life in Nazi Germany. By integrating postal materials into our study of Nazi propaganda, we will gain greater insight into the kinds of social pressures experienced by all Germans. The images and messages that Germans saw and read each and every day must have had a profound impact upon their lives and perceptions. Just as today, we Americans, see dozens of billboards and hear countless commercial messages every day designed to persuade us to purchase a particular product or service. The Germans of the 1930s and 1940s were continuously bombarded with messages glorifying militarism, endorsing racism and demanding conformity. Likewise, Germans were provided with clear and unambiguous messages as to what constituted the "good, healthy, acceptable" German of their day. While this type of phenomena existed in other nations of the time (particularly in Italy and the Soviet Union), it is my opinion that it was much more prolific and, therefore, more "poisonous" in Germany.

It is important to note that these postal materials, like all printed matter, were highly regulated by the government. We will be examining the very same messages and images that the government had approved and wanted its citizens to read and absorb. In the case of privately printed items, we will also be seeing the images that the creators thought others wanted or needed to see. Yet, even the privately printed materials were undoubtedly subjected to thorough and careful censorship in one form or another.

Also important to this discussion is the fact that the Nazi Party employed the use of postal propaganda well before coming to power. In fact, my research has uncovered examples of NSDAP (National Socialist German Worker's Party) propaganda postcards as early as 1923, months before the unsuccessful putsch of November of that same year. In addition, the subsequent imprisonment of Hitler after the putsch was characterized by a great deal of written correspondence by Hitler himself. This correspondence did much to advance the interests of the party and move it out of obscurity and into the mainstream of German politics. Knowing this, I am struck by the irony that in 1923, Hitler and his still young NSDAP could so skillfully employ the postal system of the very government they sought to destroy as a tool to carry their early propaganda messages to the nation.

My approach to this project will be largely illustrative. I will show many examples of the kinds of postal materials considered common to Germans of the day. Through my own collection and research, I have had the opportunity to see scores of postcards, postmarks, stamps and postal covers of Nazi Germany. I will refrain from boring the reader with details regarding the philatelic aspects of the illustrated material. Instead, I will focus on the propaganda and social significance of the items.

I want to make it clear that I am not an expert when it comes to the German language. In those instances where I have translated the German phrases found on the postal materials, I have done so with the aim of conveying the gist of the message. In some cases this may not constitute a precise or "perfect" translation. However, I believe that my translations assist in conveying the intended meaning of the original writer.

I will begin my discussion with an overview of the development of the postal system. Here, I will explain and illustrate the common themes of postal materials prevalent during pre-Nazi Germany as well. Next, I will show the "stage being set" for the use of postal materials as propaganda. I will then compare the propaganda methods of World War Two with previous periods in history. For example, I believe that the contrasting images of German patriotic themes in World War One vs. those of World War Two are quite striking. Finally, I will turn my attention to a discussion of materials used during the actual Nazi era: 1933-1945. At this time, I will share my opinions and observations regarding the historical and social significance of the postal materials of this time period. I will also seek to draw some conclusions regarding the intent and theoretical effect of such material. In addition, I will examine the evolution of these images and attempt to answer several key questions: What messages did the Party wish to send and at what times? How did the events of the period reflect themselves in postal material? How would one's impressions of events have been likely to develop and even change over time?

I believe that these postal materials are much more than just memorabilia. They were intended to be a significant catalyst in helping to shape public opinion. After all, the shaping of public opinion was nearly as important a task in Nazi Germany as the expansion of its territory. In fact, World War Two propaganda has been referred to as "the fourth front of warfare, comparing its strategic importance to military campaigns, diplomatic negotiations, and economic sanctions." By examining this "fourth front" of warfare, we can gain a much better understanding of how Hitler came to power and exercised that power. This book is designed to do just that by providing a careful examination of postal materials of both pre-Nazi and Nazi Germany that so permeated the day to day lives of all German citizens.[2]

CHAPTER ONE

The Development of Postal Agencies and Materials

For hundreds of years a postal system has been considered to be one of the hallmarks of an advanced society. Even ancient civilizations utilized couriers and messengers to carry important information across great distances. Today the roads of ancient Rome, or those of the Aztecs or Incas, still bear witness to the importance of such forms of long-distance communications.[1] In more recent times, national governments have created postal systems that collect postal fees from senders or recipients in return for forwarding a letter or package to a designated recipient.

Until the mid-1800s letters were usually stamped with an ink stamp and "posted" at the sender's local post office. This hand stamp certified that the necessary postage had been paid thus allowing for delivery.[2] By the 1800s most major nations had a statutory governmental postal monopoly that generated enough revenue to allow the government to pay for the service. While many nations allowed local or private couriers to carry mail (particularly in rural areas), most discovered that a monopoly was necessary in order to make their postal service economically viable.

Great Britain is actually credited with producing the first adhesive postage stamp in 1840.[3] One can also credit (or blame) her for generating the first nationalistic image on a postage stamp as that very first stamp bore an image of the then young Queen Victoria. Quickly, the entire British Empire was covered with these royal images. In fact, Britain would portray nothing other than the image of Victoria on its stamps until after her death.[4]

The postal story was much different in Germany during the 1840s for she was not yet united as a nation. The first "German" adhesive postage stamps were issued by Bavaria in 1849. Prussia followed in 1850, and most other German States and principalities issued their first stamps during the 1850s, too. Ironically, these early German stamps were largely benign with regard to national symbols and images. In fact, most of these issues by the German States merely showed numerals of value or local coats of arms. Prussia and Saxony seemed to be the exceptions with Prussia depicting King Frederick Wilhelm IV and Saxony picturing King Friedrich August II or Johann I of Saxony on their first issues.

After unification in 1871, German stamps simply portrayed the German eagle or numerals of value. Later, from 1889 to 1920, stamps bore an allegorical representation of the female "Germania." While Kaiser Wilhelm II was a popular subject of privately issued photo postcards, he never permitted his image to appear on any government issued stamps, postal cards or stationery. So, for over fifty years, Germany did not seek to glorify any individual or convey anything but the most benign propaganda message on its official postal material.[5]

Beginning in 1933, the Ministry of Post was run by Wilhelm Ohnesorge. Ohnesorge was a fanatical Nazi who had been a member of the party since the very early date of 1920.[6] This fact gives one some indication that the Nazis considered it important to make sure that this department was in politically reliable hands. Under Hitler's leadership, the post office was considered a cabinet level department on equal organizational footing with the Ministry of Foreign Affairs or the Ministry of Justice. By 1938, the post office had 300,000 employees and an annual budget of one and one half billion Reichsmarks.[7]

The development of postcards is another important aspect of this study. Heinrich von Stephan, the "Secret Councillor" of the Prussian Post, is credited with having the idea of printing postcards.[8] His idea was later promoted by Professor Dr. Emmanuel Herman of Vienna who published an article in the daily paper endorsing the introduction of postcards. The Austrian government was actually the first to accept this concept, and the first postcard was born in October of 1869. A few months later, in 1870, Germany, too, introduced her first postcards. This form of communication played an important role during the First and Second World Wars. "The reasons for this were that they made it possible to write a short message quickly, and also because the censors preferred them."[9]

Many early postcards displayed photographs of towns, monuments or architectural landmarks. Even after her victory in the Franco-Prussian War and subsequent unification, Germany's early postcards rarely portrayed nationalistic or militaristic images. An excellent example of this can be seen in this art nouveau postcard from the East Prussian town of Tilsit (below). The card portrays a portrait of Queen Luise of Prussia who met Napoleon at Tilsit in 1806-07.[10] The house in which she stayed is also shown along with the Tilsit coat of arms. Period appropriate art nouveau graphics attempt to tie these images together along with the message "Greetings from Tilsit."

Most postcards of the period, however, were simply created to send greetings from a particular place. In the late 19th century and early 20th century, photography was still new and exciting to people. In Germany, as in the rest of the world, photography made it possible to show distant friends and loved ones the place where the sender was visiting or living. Often such cards even included a hand scrawled arrow or circle identifying the particular room or apartment in which the sender was staying.

Receipt of these exotic greetings from faraway cities or villages was no doubt an exciting event. Even the actual process of photographing these postcards must have caused quite a stir in these small towns. The postcard from Gumbinnen on the next page, documents how the arrival of the photographer attracted the curiosity of a young woman and a newspaper seller who were to be forever immortalized in this postcard.

Tilsit postcard featuring Queen Luise. (No information about photographer or publisher appears on postcard.) *Author's Collection.*

Postcard of Gumbinnen Street Scene. Published by Verlag von Gustav Willudt, Gumbinnen. *Author's Collection.*

Another important aspect of this discussion of the development of postal materials is that Germany was the home of the first printing press. This fact allowed her to quickly gain high esteem in the early postcard industry. Germany's advanced level of development in the world of printed materials was such that even during the late 19th and early 20th centuries, she produced postcards for many other parts of the world including the United States. A good example of Germany's ability to combine her high quality printing techniques with the art of novelty can be seen in the card from the Rhein River region on pages 15-16. Here, the card's recipient would lift up a flap to reveal a series of photographs of the Mainz area.

The postcard on page 17 demonstrates the popularity of the German postcard industry abroad as illustrated by this beautiful, gilt postcard depicting the Abraham Lincoln home in Springfield, Illinois. This card, bearing a 1910 date on the reverse, reveals the high quality found in German-made cards. This quality was superior to those produced in the United States and elsewhere at the time. Furthermore, it was apparently sufficiently economical to have such cards printed in Germany rather than domestically.

Another prolific genre for pre-World War One German postcards were "naval" cards. These postcards were often mailed by passengers aboard ship and portrayed images of the sender's vessel. The cards both served as a means to promote a

Novelty postcard of child in nightgown. (No information about artist or publisher appears on postcard.) *Author's Collection.*

Novelty postcard with pictures pulled out of nightgown opening. (No information about artist or publisher appears on postcard.) *Author's Collection.*

German made postcard of Abraham Lincoln's home. Published by International Art Publishing Company, Berlin. *Author's Collection.*

particular steamship line for travelers as well as to convey the sender's greetings back home. At the turn of the century, Germany possessed an enormous civilian fleet that conveyed millions of passengers to ports all over the world including many, if not most, of the scores of German immigrants headed for North America. The postcard below shows the image of the steamer "Cassel" of the North German Lloyd Line. It was mailed in 1907. (This author's grandmother actually arrived in the United States aboard this very ship!)

Other postcards illustrated exotic ports of call or the luxurious accommodations found inside the German liners as documented in the two illustrations opposite. The top illustration reveals the image of a scene near Lisbon, Portugal on a card created for the exclusive use of guests of the North German Lloyd Line. The bottom card portrays an image of the posh interior of the Hamburg-America liner "Moltke."

Certainly, one could not claim that postcards such as these portray any kind of overt nationalistic images. Yet, when one considers that many of these cards were intended for foreign consumption, they do convey a certain image of Germany as a nation with advanced naval technology whose ships visited all parts of the world. This commercial attempt to convey a controlled image could be considered one of the first steps toward the use of postal materials to promote official propaganda.

One also detects a certain pride on the part of Germany and the shipping lines when viewing these naval cards. In fact, by the outbreak of World War One, it was

Postcard of the steamship "Cassel." Photographed by Albert Rosenthal, Bremen. *Author's Collection.*

Above: Postcard for use by passengers of the North German Lloyd Line. Published by Drezel and Adler, Hamburg. *Author's Collection.*

Right: Postcard of dining room on board the "Moltke" Hamburg-American Line. Published by M. and J., Hamburg. *Author's Collection.*

Colorful postcard of German military parade with message, "Greetings from the Kaiser Parade." Published by Verlag A. Franz, Leipzig. *Author's Collection.*

Postcard with photograph of Hussar Regimental Band, 1903. Photograph by Druck von F. Kemnitz, Eberswalde. *Author's Collection.*

thought that primarily because of the growth in shipping, Germany's international trade was on the verge of passing that of Great Britain. "Germany's share of world trade had grown rapidly. In 1880, Britain's share was 23%, Germany's 9%. In 1913, it was 17% and 12%."[11] It would not be lost on future generations of Germans that most of these very ships were either lost or destined to be turned over to the victorious allies after World War One as part of Germany's war reparations.

However, it would be inaccurate to assume that military themes were completely absent during the pre-World War One period. In fact, some emphasis on nationalism and militarism could be found. When military postal images of this period did appear, they were generally of a somewhat sentimental and benign nature. As mentioned earlier, postage stamps still failed to reflect any marshal images. Instead, it is the postcards that best captured the flavor of the military images of the period. The two postcards opposite illustrate this point.

The top is a colorful and attractive card that includes the embossed profiles of the Kaiser and Kaiserin on the lower right corner. While this scene does evoke an image of great national pride, it is probably not a card that could be classified as overtly propagandistic or menacing and would have been an appropriate souvenir for even a foreign visitor to mail to their home country at that time.

The bottom postcard of this period reflects the sender's pride in a particular military unit. Here, the photograph captures the image of a military band in 1903. While not a uniquely German phenomena, this "pride of membership" in a soldier's military unit is evidenced throughout German history and will be seen in World War One and World War Two. In fact, Germany's desire to create an almost tangible sense of cohesiveness and belonging is later seen as a key element in German military activities in both subsequent wars. In a related way, Hitler's theme of "volksgemeinschaft" (national community) was seen as an outgrowth of the kind of World War One military "comradeship" he, himself, had experienced while serving in the German army.

CHAPTER TWO

World War One Postal Propaganda

The development of photography was a powerful force when coupled with Germany's high level of technical expertise in the production of postcards. These two advancements seemed to set the stage for Germany to express a measure of its World War One patriotic fervor as well as propaganda through the medium of post cards. As was the case prior to the outbreak of war, the official government issues of stamps and postal cards continued to offer little in the way of officially sanctioned military or nationalistic propaganda. However, one begins to see a new resource for postal propaganda with the development of field post mail. As with most belligerent nations, Germany was compelled to develop a system of "feldpost" (field post mail) for the use of her troops. Germany boasted a very efficient system that allowed soldiers in the field to send mail home free of charge. Usually, merely writing "feldpost" in longhand was sufficient to send a card, letter or package on its way from the war front to the home front.

Soon to follow was the creation of special cards specifically designed for the use of the soldiers. These postcards were sometimes used to send home sanitized images of battle scenes. Great effort was taken to select pleasant and "peaceful" scenes to portray the early stages of this war. The card shown opposite, "Greetings from the West," makes the western front look quaint and rather uneventful. The card includes photos of livestock and "locals" posing for the German camera. This early practice of filtering the images of war set the stage for the later all-out

Postcard with photographs of four pastoral scenes from the western front, 1914-1915. Photograph by Druck: Korner and Lauterbach, Chemnitz. *Author's Collection.*

propaganda campaign that was skillfully designed to shape public opinion about the next war. After all, how could a mother *possibly* lose a moment of sleep knowing her son was in a charming place like this?

Naturally, another favorite theme for postcards during this early World War One period was the display of enemy prisoners. The feldpost card on the following page showed the folks back home the image of a trainload of captured Frenchmen. Here one sees a chance meeting of French and German soldiers presumably moving in opposite directions. French troops were headed into captivity in open train cars while Germans in covered train cars were headed for the front. The amount of detail shown in these old photos is amazing. For example, close inspection reveals that the Frenchmen are in coal cars belonging to the Royal Saxony Railroad Company. Despite its unification in 1872, Germany was still subject to such regional distinctions. Nonetheless, standardized railroad gauges made it possible for Saxon train cars to be used in the war effort far to the west.

While it may have been lost on many of the recipients of these cards, the intended message of victory and efficiency seems evident today. Here, victory is represented by the image of captured prisoners, and efficiency is represented by the documentation of this train (so far from its official home) being used for the war effort. This postcard was likely designed to create a sense of awe over the

Begegnung gef. Franzosen u. deutscher Soldaten

Postcard with photograph of German soldiers and French prisoners aboard passing trains. Photograph by Hans Hidenbrand, Stuttgart. *Author's Collection.*

success Germany was then enjoying while simultaneously demonstrating the vastness of Germany's resources.

Another significant style of postcard was being produced during this period. This type focused on portraying an almost romantic side of war as seen in the example shown opposite. One is especially struck by the *amount* of sentimentality and gut wrenching pathos frequently found with this type of German World War One postcard. This postcard genre clearly emphasized the pain and separation of war, yet simultaneously romanticized the image of the soldier. And while these images were usually draped in the imperial colors or accompanied by an iron cross, they could hardly be described as "warlike."

The card on page 26 illustrates this romantic image. Here, the iron cross is combined with a message of nationalism. In this illustration, one sees not just a representation of the fierce leader, Hindenburg, but an almost loving tribute to him as, "Our Hindenburg."

The final card illustrating this genre of propaganda (page 27) is an extremely blatant example of this emotion grabbing style. This card depicts a soldier sitting on a moss-covered rock as he pauses to read a letter presumably from his wife or girlfriend. He is certainly not portrayed to be a fierce, rugged soldier. In fact, he has actually put down his gun in order to pick some spring flowers. The sentimentality represented in this card is tremendous.

Postcard combining romantic and patriotic themes with romantic poem, "It Was in the Silvery Moonlight." (No information about publisher, author or artist appears on postcard.) *Author's Collection.*

Postcard with photograph of German General, Von Hindenburg. Photograph by Rotophot, A.-G., Berlin. *Author's Collection.*

Postcard of soldier dreaming of his beloved with the message, "Happy Pentecost." (No information about publisher or artist appears on postcard.) *Author's Collection.*

These are hardly the images of "war" one would expect to see based upon one's knowledge of the history of World War One. Yet, they are very typical of the cards that millions of civilians received from German soldiers serving on the front. Furthermore, these kinds of cards stand in stark contrast to those later seen in World War Two. And while "Unser Hindenburg" (our Hindenburg) later evolves into "Unser Fuhrer" (our leader), one hardly sees anything like these from Germany in the war to come. This is not to say that Germany eschewed nationalist propaganda in World War One. Instead, the propaganda used thus far seems to have been aimed mostly at romanticizing war and presenting sanitized images of soldiers' lives. Presumably, the government sought to gain civilian approval in this way. Although many cards give glimpses of military scenes, one does not see portrayals of the *reality* of war as the fighting man would have seen it. Instead, compared to what is to follow in World War Two, the propaganda examined thus far seems rather amateurish and almost comical.

The card opposite is entitled, "The First Flag Captured at Luneville on August 11, 1914." With this card, one sees an attempt to actually convey a more realistic glimpse of battle. Portrayed is one of Germany's earliest engagements with France that occurred during the first few days of the war. The work seeks to glorify the victorious Germans and shows the highly "sanitized" images of dead Frenchmen.

August 1914 was also the beginning of another, even more historically significant, battle *inside* Germany. This was the time when Russia invaded the province of East Prussia and threatened even the old Imperial city of Koenigsberg. The subsequent battle of Tannenberg, represented a significant German victory against superior numbers. The successful leadership of Hindenburg in this battle contributed to his growing popularity among his countrymen as we have seen. This "eastern victory" became a favorite theme of postcards at the time as evidenced in the next two illustrations shown on page 30.

The top card titled, "The Capture of Russian Ulans in Battle in East Prussia" celebrates this stunning accomplishment. The bottom card is an even more comprehensive portrayal of this victory. It was mailed as a field post card by a soldier in 1916 and exhibits the victorious figure of Hindenburg standing over a fallen Russian bear. The air is filled with "state of the art" biplanes and a zeppelin. The skies have cleared as symbolized by the glowing sun, and in the distant background, one can make out images of some of the major cities of the German Prussian east, Koenigsberg, Graudenz, Thorn, Posen and Breslau.

Postcard with sketch of German victory at Luneville on August 11, 1914. Published by Leunis-Verlag, Berlin. *Author's Collection.*

Postcard with sketch of Germans and Russians in battle in East Prussia. Artwork by Curtschulz, Steglistz. Published by K.V., Berlin. *Author's Collection.*

Postcard with allegory of German victory in the East. Published by A. Kosel, Lugau. *Author's Collection.*

Russische Parade in Insterburg am 3. Sept. 1914.
1. General Rennenkampf,
2. Großfürst Nicolai
nehmen den Parademarsch ab.

Postcard with photograph of Rennenkampf and Nicoli reviewing the Russian troops on parade in Insterburg, Germany on September 3, 1914. Published by Verlag R. Gottwaldt, Insterburg. *Author's Collection.*

The next two highly fascinating postcards from this era are representative of a slightly different subject matter. In order to better understand these scenes, it is helpful to recall some background information regarding the events that they document.

The German city of Insterburg was right in the path of the advancing Russian army. For a period of several days this city, like many of its neighboring cities, was under Russian occupation. Knowing this, one wonders *why* Germans would choose to commemorate a piece of history that clearly represented a loss for their cause. For several days, this city was taken over by hostile forces and held by Russian troops.

In the card shown on page 31, Russian troops are shown marching into the town of Insterburg. The card marks this event as having occurred on September 3, 1914. It also documents the presence of Russian Generals Rennenkampf and Nicolai reviewing the troops. This comprehensive photograph seems to capture every detail of this historic moment.

The card below entitled, "Retreat of the Last Russian Troops at Insterburg," shows the same Russian soldiers as they retreated through the streets of the city. Here, even the time of their departure at 2:30 in the afternoon was recorded. Again

Postcard with photograph of retreat of Russian troops from Insterburg, Germany on September 11, 1914. Published by Verlag R. Gottwaldt, Insterburg. *Author's Collection.*

the vivid and well-focused photography puts the viewer right into the scene. One can even read the signs of the businesses lining the streets of Insterburg.

While the German recipients of this second card might have taken pride in the fact that the Russians were forced to retreat, by later standards it is remarkable that either of these cards would ever have been created. For these cards not only illustrate the events in Insterburg, they leave little room for interpretation since they are actual photographs. An enterprising photographer both immortalized these scenes and provided us with enduring records of these monumental events. These photos captured the wartime occupation of a German city by hostile forces now forever frozen in time.

Numerous other examples of somewhat surprising choices of subject matter can also be found. The card below is just one of many cards printed to show the damage caused by Russian troops occupying East Prussia. The photograph reveals the devastation found in the aftermath of artillery bombardment on a Tilsit mill. Again one sees images of a German military and property loss.

A similar postcard on the next page reads: "How the Russians Wreaked Havoc in East Prussia." It portrays the interior of one of the many businesses vandalized during the Russian occupation in East Prussia. It is interesting to note that this card was postmarked in November 1914. This means a soldier mailed it home at least

Postcard with photograph of the ruins at Tilsit, Germany on September 13, 1914. Published by Verlag and Eigentum, Litauen. *Author's Collection.*

Postcard with photograph of interior of ransacked business in East Prussia, 1914. Published by Gustav Liersch & Co., Berlin. *Author's Collection.*

two to three months *before* East Prussia was entirely free of Russian troops. Therefore, this postcard was being produced and circulated before Germany could have known the ultimate fate of this occupied portion of Germany.

Perhaps Germany justified the irony of producing such postcards bearing images of East Prussian destruction for economic reasons. Such cards were usually sold with a surcharge to supplement the cost of reconstruction. Or, perhaps Germany failed to even consider the ironies found here. In retrospect, it seems truly remarkable that these images were ever used for postcards. They attest to Germany's early defeats and the Russian incursion onto German territory. Though it can also be said that they seek to represent a certain anti-Russian element by their stark portrayal of what the German population saw as Russian "barbarism."

The fact remains that Germany did permit the creation of a huge variety of postal cards and materials during World War One. Yet, in this study of propaganda, one will come to realize that such cards lacked the "menacing" sort of military or nationalist propaganda found in World War Two. While they blandly sought to glorify certain military engagements or convey pro-German patriotic sentiment, they also did not differ greatly from the materials offered up by other nations of the day.

CHAPTER THREE

German Postal Materials After World War One

The period between the end of World War One and 1933 was not particularly remarkable for German postal history. During this time Germany, like many other nations, enjoyed a flowering of artistic and cultural expression that sometimes found its way onto German postal materials. There were, however, two very significant issues which made the postal material of the interwar period highly significant and worthy of discussion. The first was the creation of separate postal issues for each of the "plebiscite" areas. These areas, designated by the Treaty of Versailles, would vote on whether to remain part of Germany or join other countries. The second significant issue during the interwar period was Germany's experience with hyperinflation. These two influential events were seen reflected in the postal material of the day and were eventually burned into the memory of every German man, woman and child who lived through these trying years.

It would be a gross oversimplification to imply that the entire postal history of Germany in the period from 1918 to 1933 could be summed up with a discussion of the plebiscite issues and the inflation. Many other types of postal material existed. For example, during this time period, the first airmail stamps were issued (including those carried on the dramatic zeppelin flights), and the first "semi-postal" stamps were issued (where extra money was paid to support a national cause). There were even some postal cards and materials issued by nationalist and anti-Semitic groups which foreshadowed the later themes of the Nazis.

35

However, much of the development of postal materials in this period was influenced by actual events. Virtually nothing could have had as much impact on German life as witnessing the nation being cut apart and experiencing the economy slide into total collapse. "Millions of Germans saw the apparently solid framework of their existence cracking and crumbling."[1] This "cracking and crumbling" was soon viewed by large numbers of Germans as evidence that their new republican form of government was incapable of maintaining order. This growing skepticism led to negative comparisons of their current government with the monarchy that had preceded it.

It was this atmosphere that allowed a man like Hitler and a political movement such as the National Socialists to look very attractive to large segments of this exhausted and fearful nation. "In such circumstances men entertain fantastic fears, extravagant hatreds, and extravagant hopes. In such circumstances the extravagant demagogy of Hitler began to attract a mass following as it had never done before."[2]

Although the atmosphere was right for Hitler's ascension to power, the nation needed to become better acquainted with what, at first glance, might have seemed to many to be just *another* band of political extremists and crackpots. Dozens of such groups existed in Germany at that time. Hitler must have recognized this. What better way could there have been for millions to become "acquainted" with this movement than through the mail? The German citizens' daily visit to their mailbox represented a golden opportunity for Hitler to imprint images and messages of this new political movement on the minds these citizens. "Hitler's use of propaganda, if not necessarily his most effective weapon, was certainly his most sinister. . . persuading the Germans that the Nazi system would restore their country's greatness."[3]

At the end of World War One many Germans also felt a strong sense of betrayal and injustice. These people were described as having a "deep hostility towards the failed democratic system. . . and a widespread feeling. . . that Germany had been badly wronged at Versailles."[4] Life was very different for German citizens following this war. Their homeland was being cut up into seemingly countless pieces as vast amounts of territory were reassigned to other nations. After nearly 50 years, Alsace and Lorraine (which Germany had gained in the Franco Prussian War) were now returned to France. Extensive amounts of eastern territory, too, were assigned to the newly created Polish state including many major cities such as Posen (the birthplace of Hindenburg) and Bromberg. Even the tiny region around the towns of Eupen and Malmedy was annexed to Belgium, and the ancient Hanseatic trading city of Danzig and its surrounding area were designated as a "free city" or a virtual nation unto itself. Likewise, the town and region of Memel, in Germany's far northeast, were taken under League of Nations control and eventually passed to the newly created nation of Lithuania. In addition, several more jurisdictions were identified as areas where votes would be taken to decide the fate of the territory. These were Allenstein and Marienwerder in East Prussia, which would decide between Poland and Germany. Silesia in the southeast was to decide between Poland and Germany, and Schleswig (on the border with Denmark) was to decide between Germany and Denmark. The Saar region was soon occupied by France and become a separate postal area for purposes of issuing stamps and postage materials. Yes, Germany was disintegrating as new nations were emerging and new territories were assigned. Her people and her lands were being split apart. The resulting postal material would bear witness to these situations.

Although there was a certain ethnic mixture in these plebiscite areas, ordinary Germans had grown up thinking of these towns and regions as unquestionably German in character, and of course, even the ethnic non-Germans living in such areas had fought *with* Germany in the war as German citizens since birth.[5] It must have come as quite a shock then, when a German received an envelope, such as this from an old friend or relative in Memel. A close examination reveals just how startling this must have been. First, the League of Nations officials chose to create "new" stamps out of French stamps by overprinting the name "Memel" and a new

Envelope with overprinted French postage stamps for use in the Memel region. Memel (League of Nations) postal authority. *Author's Collection.*

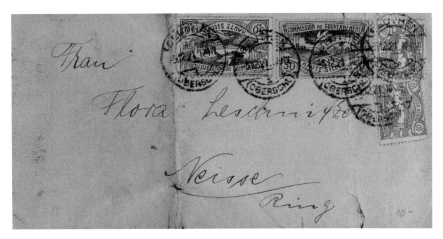

Envelope with postage stamps for Upper Silesia. Plebiscite (Silesian) postal authority. *Author's Collection.*

denomination over the original French markings. Furthermore, one must realize that at this time the German anthem, "Deutschland Uber Alles," contained the lyrics, "from the Maas to the Memel," in its familiar, well memorized lines. The recipient of this mail in Chemnitz surely did not fail to notice the perhaps inadvertent or careless insult derived from these stamps.

Similarly, a letter from the Upper Silesian town of Beuthen in 1921 (above) bears stamps from the League of Nations Government for Silesia. Again, stamps were created especially for the region. Yet, here the entire stamp was printed in French! This is remarkable since there were virtually no French speakers in the entire region, or for that matter, even among the workers in the local postal service. The recipient of this letter was a resident of Silesia who undoubtedly must have found the letter from her own province a bit of a curiosity, if not an outright insult. Seemingly minor issues such as these, played well into the propaganda program of the era's demagogues.

Similar stamps and postal items were issued in the areas of Allenstein, Marienwerder and Schleswig, all of which would hold plebiscites. The crucial elections to be held in these regions became another arena for postal materials. Examples of this are seen in the next two noteworthy propaganda postcards from Silesia issued to publicize their upcoming vote (opposite). The top card urges the reader to, "Remember the vote in Upper Silesia on 20 March 1921." Across the top it reads, "Unity, a strong bond, holds together people and land." This particular card appears to have been hand drawn. The artist rendered images of the local coal

Above: Postcard with slogan urging voters not to forget the Upper Silesian Plebiscite. (No information about publisher or artist appears on postcard.) *Author's Collection.*

Right: Pro-German propaganda post-card for the Upper Silesian Plebiscite. (No information about publisher or artist appears on postcard.) *Author's Collection.*

mines and a miner. Although it bears no identification as to where it might have been printed or who drew the images, it does contain their sentiment. This is revealed with the words "good luck" in German appearing over the coal mine. The reverse of the card reveals a postmark from the town of Tarnowitz, which became a part of Poland after the vote.

The bottom card also appears to have been privately produced but displays somewhat more professional looking graphics. This card was postmarked in the town of Peiskretscham which voted to remain German. The face of the card displays the arms of the major cities of the region and features an image of "Germania" with cherubs holding a ballot box. The heavy industry of the region is symbolized along with two figures. One is a worker and the other is perhaps a policeman or military man. The messages again are in German and read: "Be United-United-United" and "We want to be a united people of brothers."

The result of the Silesian plebiscite was likely somewhat disappointing to both Germans and Poles. The eastern part, including the significant cities of Kattowitz, Myslowitz, Rybnik, Tarnowitz and Lublinitz, passed to Polish control while the larger western portion remained part of Germany. Elsewhere, Allenstein voted to remain entirely German as did Marienwerder. The northern portion of Schleswig voted to join Denmark while the southern part remained German. Even in those areas that remained under German control, a stark reminder of the "humiliating" terms of the Treaty of Versailles could be seen by nationalistic Germans in the postal issues of these so-called plebiscite states.

A slightly different variation was found in the case of Danzig. This city was thought to hold the key to both the Baltic Sea and the mouth of the Vistula River. Therefore, it was determined that, despite the German majority in the city, it must not remain under German control lest it threaten the newly independent Poland. It was considered essential that Poland have access to the Baltic Sea. Therefore, the mostly German city of Danzig and a mostly Polish hinterland were joined to form a "free city" patterned after a similar arrangement that existed during one period of Danzig's ancient past. Danzig became a separate postal issuing entity and a virtually independent nation. Her postal issues were printed in the German language, and the area remained largely German in character. But, as the 1930s progressed, Danzig gained a particularly large number of Nazi Party members and sympathizers among her citizens who eventually controlled the government of the "free city." This postal card (opposite) illustrates how Danzig initially overprinted German stamp stock, but began printing its own issues as the supply was used. The city of Danzig and its

Postcard with German stamps overprinted "Danzig." Danzig postal authority. *Author's Collection.*

surrounding area remained independent until 1939 when rejoined with Germany by force.[6]

German bitterness over the loss of so much territory, and the Nazi's ability to make a propaganda issue out of it, significantly helped to fuel Hitler's popularity among German nationalists and right-wingers. In addition, the "liberation" of Danzig was used as one pretext for the attack against Poland in September of 1939. Further upheaval came during 1922 and 1923 as Germany experienced a period of hyperinflation. This meant that the stamps necessary to merely mail a postcard or letter would require the expenditure of sums of money which just months before would have represented an individual's entire life's savings! By the end of this period of hyperinflation, the government was forced to print postage stamps denominated in trillions of marks just to mail a letter. This crisis was one of the most traumatic and memorable stages in pre-Nazi postal history.

The next postcard on page 42, purchased by an American tourist in Berlin, was sent during this remarkable era and required an astonishing 36,000 marks to be mailed! The visitor's hand-written message focuses on this economic crisis. She writes, "We are still struggling with millions here and spend about 1/3 of our time in counting our money. We got 5,500,000 marks today for $1.00 but we find everything is twice as high this year and the stock is low of nearly everything." The card was written on August 27, 1923.

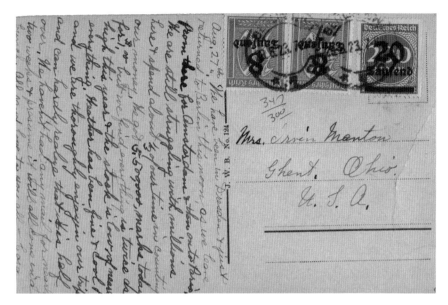

Postcard from American tourists with thirty six thousand Marks in postage. Published by J.W.G. #124. *Author's Collection.*

By mid-November of that same year, Germany's currency value had declined to a staggering 1.3 trillion marks to the dollar. A ten million mark banknote of the era is shown opposite. It was this catastrophic inflation that served both to undermine German citizens' confidence in their new democratic form of government as well as literally destroy their lives and spirits. This is summed up best in the words of Otto Friedrich:

> The fundamental quality of the disaster was a complete loss of faith in the functioning of society. Money is important not just as a medium of exchange, after all, but as a standard by which society judges our work, and thus our selves. If all money becomes worthless, then so does all government, and all society, and all standards. In the madness of 1923, a workman's work was worthless, a widow's savings were worthless, everything was worthless.[7]

It was no coincidence, then, that Hitler chose November of 1923 for his infamous and unsuccessful Beer Hall Putsch. While Friedrich wrote that the inflation represented "the real revolution"[8] of that year, he went on to say, "The whole nation, tired of war, actually longed only for order."[9] Assuming Friedrich's summation is accurate, it is not surprising that Hitler's motley band of revolutionaries failed in their attempt to seize power that November and was years away from any semblance of public acceptance. Later, "restoration of order" became one of Hitler's major and most popularly received themes.

In that same year of 1923, one finds the first propaganda postcard offerings of the young Nazi party as well. However, they had very little circulation and were considered to be rather crude. The Nazis perfected the art within the next ten years, however. The card on page 44 is representative of this early, unrefined stage.

It should also be noted that during this time period postcards and various forms of postal material such as labels or stickers became increasingly popular with many political parties. Nationalists, Communists, Social Democrats, as well as the Nazis, used postcards to get out their messages. However, the available literature indicates that the Nazis, in particular, used extremely colorful and powerful "patriotic" images on postal cards beginning in 1930.

These eye-catching postcards were used as election propaganda and were even passed out at polling places. Favorite themes included Hitler's image, pictures of the Nazi "martyr," Horst Wessel and the words and music to the Horst Wessel Song (the Nazi's anthem). This was also the time when postcards began to appear with rather crude, but powerful, anti-Semitic images portraying Jews as international conspirators, moneygrubbers and communists. These images were cynically designed to categorize Jewish men and women as the richly dressed, arrogant and

Ten million Mark banknote dated August 1923. German government. *Author's Collection.*

One of the earliest NSDAP propaganda postcards seeking to link Nazi storm troops with Germany's past.
Reprinted by permission of R. J. Bender Publishing.

hook-nosed creators of Germany's misfortune in nearly every aspect of public and economic life. The Nazi "good guys" were often shown running them out of town in such portrayals.

However, it should also be noted that these postal materials were the propaganda creations of an "out of power" party. Once the Nazis gained power in 1933, even party issued cards or private ones obtained virtual official status due to the rapid Nazi consolidation of power. Once the Nazis assumed power and consolidated their control, virtually nothing could be printed, much less mailed, without the approval of the national or regional governments. Therefore, in the chapters to follow, it is important to bear in mind that the postal materials created *after* the Nazis came to power necessarily required the government's "blessing" for their very existence. In addition, the creators and senders of even private material knew that every item would be noticed and reviewed by the "powers that be."

CHAPTER FOUR

The Early Years of Nazi Rule

The Consolidation of Power

The earliest days of Nazi rule in Germany were characterized by two rather contradictory strategies. The first was a desire on the part of the Nazis to make the transfer of power as smooth as possible. This strategy was designed to ease the concerns of conservatives, nationalists, military leaders, and business people whose support the Nazis believed they needed. Many of these groups had already begun lending financial and political support to the Nazis whom they saw as a more acceptable alternative than the SPD (Social Democratic Party of Germany) or the KPD (Communist Party of Germany). The Nazis would not have lasted long if they had gained a reputation as radicals akin to that of the Communists or Socialists in the minds of German conservatives.

At the same time, however, it was essential to the Nazis that their consolidation of power proceed as *quickly* as possible. This desire for a quick transition certainly made it difficult to maintain the appearance of non-radicalism. These conflicting strategies were clearly evidenced in the early postal history of the Nazi regime.

Hitler rapidly began wielding his influence on postal related materials. Gone were the postal materials admitting to territorial loss and damage. Gone were the cards depicting "sanitized" battle scenes or "romantic" portrayals of soldiers picking flowers while dreaming of far off girlfriends. Hitler had no intention of continuing this subtle type of propaganda because he was convinced of the failure of his country's World War One propaganda. "It need not surprise us that our propaganda did not enjoy. . . success. In our ambiguity alone, it bore the germ of ineffectual-ness."[1] Not only did Hitler realize the failure of previous propaganda (including presumably, postal propaganda), he realized its incredible potential. This realization was echoed in the words of Hitler, "But it was not until the War that it became evident what immense results could be obtained by a correct application of propaganda."[2]

It was to his advantage that in 1927, Germany issued a series of stamps bearing the faces of German Presidents. This series included a stately image of Hindenburg and marked the first time a living political figure had ever been portrayed on a German stamp or official postal item. Throughout Hitler's early years, the Hindenburg image remained a popular theme. After all, Hindenburg's appointment of Hitler as Chancellor provided the otherwise "revolutionary" Nazis with an aura of legitimacy. Maintaining his portrait on stamps and postcards served as a subtle reminder of this fact. Furthermore, Hindenburg's reputation as the victor of the Battle of Tannenberg gave his image even further significance and popular appeal.

The card seen below is one example from a huge series of cards issued between 1932 and the early 1940s. The title on the upper left translates roughly: "Learn to

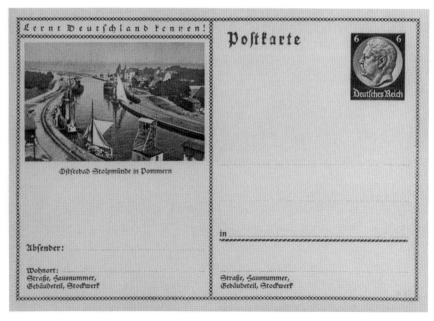

Postcard featuring the Baltic Sea resort of Stolpmunde in Pomerania from the "Get to Know Germany" series. German postal authority. *Author's Collection.*

Know Germany." It portrays the Baltic Sea resort of Stolpmuende in the province of Pomerania, now in Poland. This series of postcards carried pictures of hundreds of scenes and attractions within Germany. It is important to note that the first versions of this series carried the portrait of President Ebert in 1932. From 1933-1941, this same series displayed Hindenburg's portrait, and from 1941 on, Hindenburg's image was replaced with Hitler's.

This is perhaps one of the best examples of Hitler's cunning ability to manipulate. In this case it was a manipulation of postal images. He was able to take the postcards already in use and slowly, cleverly evolve them into a tool of Nazi propaganda. The evolution of this series of cards also demonstrates the clear connection the Nazis strove to maintain with the pre-Nazi past. They were careful to maintain the exact same design as in the 1932 "Ebert" version changing only the portrait. Later, as will be shown, these same postcards even came to chronicle the progress of the war to come.

During the early months of Nazi rule, postage stamps remained relatively apolitical. For example, in November 1933, a set of stamps was created to commemorate Wagnerian operas. However, these stamps were printed on paper bearing swastika watermarks that could only be seen when held up to the light. Similarly, most stamps issued after this date were printed on such paper.

The first stamp to actually bear the image of a swastika on its face was an airmail stamp issued in 1934. This particular example of the stamp was used in 1937 and featured a special "Condor Legion Homecoming" cancellation. The Condor Legion was the German force that fought for Franco in the Spanish Civil War. The image on this stamp included the dramatic design of a "swastika sun" illuminating the world.

Airmail postage stamp with eagle and swastika rising. German postal authority. *Author's Collection.*

It is significant that Germany chose an airmail stamp to be the first stamp to bear a swastika for two reasons. First, it would not have been seen by many Germans in daily usage since airmail was a much more expensive mailing method. Second, it *would* have been seen quite often outside of Germany since airmail was frequently used for international mailings. However, as 1934 wore on, the swastika and more overt propaganda themes became much more common on nearly all official postal materials.

At the same time, "unofficial" pro-Nazi postal materials exploded beginning in January of 1933. One such unofficial postcard appears below. It portrays Frederick the Great, Bismarck, Hindenburg and Hitler. The message along the bottom translates: "What the King conquered, the ruler shaped, the field marshal defended, the soldier rescued and united." This card accomplished two important objectives of Nazi propaganda. First, it established Hitler as the successor to these towering, heroic figures of the German past. At the same time, it placed Hitler in a position of humility and commonness by describing him as a mere "soldier" in the symbolic message.

Great effort was taken during the early stages of Hitler's rise to power to make him appear to be a common man called by destiny to finish the work of the great leaders who preceded him. Evidence of the success of this early strategy can be

Postcard with drawings of four leaders: Frederick, Bismarck, Hindenburg and Hitler. Artwork by Art Institute of Johannes. Published by Boettger, Koln. *Author's Collection.*

found in this excerpt from the book, *They Thought They Were Free*: "Hitler was a man, one like ourselves, a little man, who, by doing what he did, was a testament to the democracy 'you Americans' talk about, the ability of us little men to become great and to rule the world."[3]

The next major event influencing postal propaganda was the burning of the Reichstag building in February 1933. Hitler used this catastrophe as a pretext for the consolidation of police powers under Nazi control as well as an excuse for outlawing the German Communist Party. Postcards such as the one seen opposite were created to implant images of this national landmark in ruins in the German people's minds. It is significant to note that this particular card was postmarked and mailed from Berlin to the United States on March 10, 1933. The Reichstag fire occurred on February 27, 1933. It seems remarkable that just ten or eleven days after the fire, Germans were able to purchase and mail photo postcards documenting the damage. After all, the photograph probably could not have been taken until at least February 28th or March 1st due to the intense heat and smoke that would have remained immediately after the fire. This timing of the photograph is further supported by the presence of several police or fire officials seen standing on the upper level just above the word "Plenarsaal" (assembly room). It is clear that the quick, widespread release of this effective piece of propaganda was encouraged as a tool to convey the very high significance of this event to German citizens.

Hitler's quest for power quickly gained momentum following the Reichstag fire. Less than a month later, on March 23, 1933, the Nazis succeeded in obtaining the passage of the so-called Enabling Act in a Reichstag session at Potsdam. This act, in effect, gave Hitler the power to act independently of both the President and the Reichstag on a broad range of matters.

Ironically, 1933 also marked the 10th anniversary of the Munich Beer Hall Putsch. By November of that year, dozens of different commemorative postcards were printed to mark this anniversary. The postcard on page 52 was published by Heinrich Hoffman, who later came to be known as Hitler's official photographer. This dramatic image includes photographs of the fallen "heroes" of the putsch, the plaque in their honor (which was placed at the Feldherrnhalle in Munich) and the Feldherrnhalle itself. The inscription translates: "Despite all you were victorious."

It is not difficult to imagine the dramatic impact such a piece would have had on an ordinary German living in November of 1933. The obscure, almost comical, political party of 1923 that had failed so miserably in its attempt to seize power now, literally, ran the country. Monuments and solemn quasi-religious events were

Postcard with photograph of gutted Reichstag. (No information about photographer or publisher appears on postcard.) *Author's Collection.*

Postcard with names and photographs of Nazis killed in Munich Putsch. Photograph by Heinrich Hoffman, Munich. *Author's Collection.*

even held to celebrate the sacrifice of these men who had previously been seen as troublemakers and criminals. These postcards were used to drill home the message that political dissent was now unacceptable, if not illegal. Each day, Germans were reminded of these images. This served to encourage acceptance and, eventually for many, enthusiasm for the new state of affairs in Germany. In fact, the cards became so popular that people like Hoffman became rich selling them. One must realize that his (and other sellers') customers were not just fanatical Nazis. They were also the ordinary men and women who wanted to appear to be "in step" with the new spirit of the day. The mere act of purchasing and mailing a postcard thus made it possible for a German of the day to convey his or her willingness to conform.

Hitler's power was growing and by late 1933, through the establishment of new laws (such as the Enabling Act) and the overwhelming Nazi control of the police apparatus, there was *very* strict regulation of anything that found its way into the public domain. For this reason, even privately produced postcards and postal materials were subject to removal from circulation if they deviated too much from the desired party line. At the same time, most Germans (with the obvious exception of many Jews) were at least mildly enthusiastic about their new government. Many of the postal materials of these early days, therefore, reflected that enthusiasm.

The postcard at the top of page 54 is evidence of this enthusiasm. While it is not an example of actual postal propaganda, it does contain the sender's personal form of propaganda. Careful examination of this card (mailed in December 1934) reveals the words "Heil Hitler" before the signature at end of its message. For Nazis and other Germans, the words "Heil Hitler" became the accepted form for greeting someone or for closing a card or letter. Richard Grunberger reflected on this widespread ritual: "The obligation incumbent upon all citizens to use the 'Heil Hitler!' greeting on every occasion was one of the most potent forms of totalitarian conditioning conceivable."[4]

Likewise, the subject matter of "official" stamps, postcards and even postmarks began to embrace similar Nazi enthusiasm by 1934. A particularly dramatic example of this can be seen in the official postcard shown at the bottom of page 54 (issued in January 1934), to commemorate the first anniversary of Hitler's appointment as Chancellor. This card illustrates several examples of the ongoing evolution of Nazi postal propaganda. For instance, Hitler's image was used for the very first time on an *official* piece of German postal material. Secondly, just one year after coming to power, the swastika had now expanded to become the national symbol, not just

Verden, den 1. Dez. 1934

Sehr geehrter Herr Lücken!

Antwortlich Ihrer werten Anfrage vom 29 vM.
teile ich Ihnen mit, dass die Chorstimmen zu den
Slg. Chorfreunde je 15 Pf. zu den beiden Liedern
aus dem Verlag f dt. Musik je 20 Pf. kosten. Ich
möchte daher erst anfragen, ob ich die Stimmen zu
diesen Preisen liefern darf.

Heil Hitler!

December 1934 postcard with typed message: "Heil Hitler." (No information about publisher appears on postcard.) *Author's Collection.*

Poſtkarte

6 6

Deutſches Reich

Deutſchland, Deutſchland über alles!
30. 1. 1933

Official postcard commemorating one year of Nazi rule. German postal authority. *Author's Collection.*

a party symbol. Even the illustration used here was significant. The extraordinary picture depicts thousands of jubilant Germans giving the raised arm salute to legions of "brownshirts" as they march through the Brandenburg Gate. The words of the German National Anthem appear below the image. It is also interesting to note that it was still deemed prudent to include Hindenburg's picture alongside that of Hitler. The transformation of power was almost complete; but vestiges of the evolutionary process could still be seen in this particular example. Perhaps more conservative (or more doubtful) Germans might be reassured by the concession to legality that the inclusion of the image of Hindenburg represented.

From this point forward, it is clear that the importance of postal material as a form of propaganda was fully recognized. In addition, the overall design and production quality of these materials seemed to be considerably improved. The next three examples illustrate this improved quality. The first card, shown below, was an official postal issue for the National Labor Day on May 1, 1934. It portrays a dramatic image of a laborer engulfed in a sea of swastikas. Propaganda can even be seen in the card's postal cancellation. It urges Germans to use their telephones with the slogan: "save time and money."

Postcard commemorating the May 1st holiday. German postal authority. *Author's Collection.*

One of the most striking propaganda images of 1934 was found in the stamp issued to commemorate the Nuremberg Party Congress. The stamp seen above was issued in September of that year. It is characterized by a "swastika sun" glowing behind a Nuremberg castle and was postmarked on board the ship "Hansestadt Danzig" on a trip between Sweinemuende and Pillau. The power of the sun was used as a metaphor for the power of the Nazis. Clearly viewers of this stamp were meant to recognize the overwhelming influence this regime would have on Germany in both the public and private spheres.

The third example further illustrates the rise in the quality of the work found in German postal materials. This postcard (opposite) represents an upgrade in artistic quality and boasts a very sophisticated design. Furthermore, its subject matter makes it extremely important for a variety of reasons. It was created for the "Kraft durch Freude" (strength through joy) Stamp Collectors Division and featured "The German Family Through Themes on German Postage Stamps." This card was cancelled with a special "Strength Through Joy" postmark that was prepared for the Chemnitz Stamp Collectors Organization. It is an extraordinary piece of Nazi propaganda designed to pay tribute to the "ideal" German family. This ideal family consisted of a father in the SA (brownshirts), a son in the Hitler Youth, a daughter in the League of German Girls, a grandfather figure who appears to be a war veteran, and a devoted mother figure. The mother was represented here by the 1935 stamp in which the Saarland was allegorically reunited with "mother Germany." These

Postcard commemorating the German family. German postal authority. *Author's Collection.*

images also convey an almost eerily fierce spirit of energy and determination that were also considered "ideal" characteristics of a German family.

Claims of Progress and Superiority

Another particularly significant aspect of the continuing evolution of postal propaganda was the development of the treatment of Hitler and the Nazi party. As the years passed, the messages regarding Hitler and his party increasingly sought to convey progress and success. Gone were the days when German postcards would be permitted to depict photographs documenting defeat. At this stage, the emphasis was to be placed on images of accomplishment.

For example, on the postcard at the top of page 58 one sees Hitler turning over the first spade of dirt signifying the commencement of the Autobahn construction program in September 1933. The message at the bottom celebrates the completion of 1000 kilometers of autobahn exactly three years later. German citizens who came in contact with this card surely must have marveled at the speed of such an achievement by this new leader.

As mentioned previously, crucial to Hitler's plan to achieve power, was his plan to achieve it *quickly*. This was particularly apparent in 1937. That year marked

Postcard commemorating the 3rd Anniversary of Hitler breaking ground for building of Autobahn. German postal authority. *Author's Collection.*

four years of Nazi rule in Germany. "Give me four years' time" became the Nazis' motto. The words were taken from one of Hitler's early speeches in which he declared that if given just four years time, he would transform Germany.[5] Hitler held an exhibition exactly four years after taking power to demonstrate the results of his promise. The exhibition was held in Berlin from April 20th to June 30th, 1937.

This registered letter (opposite) was post-marked at the exhibition. The sender completely covered the face of the envelope with a set of stamps issued in September 1936. The stamps themselves were even an "exhibition" of Hitler's four years of accomplishments. An image of architectural progress was boldly printed on each of the nine stamps. The message to German citizens was clear: under Nazi rule, bridges had been constructed and public buildings had been built. In short, postal propaganda was used to help Germans associate Hitler with jobs and progress.

The previous two postal items graphically illustrate a favorite technique of the regime. In both cases the items were created to show images of progress and Nazi promises kept. This propaganda was designed to stand in stark contrast to the images of deadlock and stalemate that the Nazis had so carefully cultivated with regard to prior German governments.

Envelope with nine stamps featuring German construction projects, 1937. German postal authority. *Author's Collection.*

An even more dramatic illustration of this desired image is seen on page 60 on a 1937 postcard entitled, "Our New Germany Stands for Honor and Work." This card is a significant piece of Nazi propaganda for a number of reasons. First, the card served as yet another reminder to its reader of Germany's progress in the area of employment as lines of laborers are shown with tools in hand. This image of success, however, was combined with a reminder that Germany was now experiencing a return of "honor." The military image at the top of the card left little doubt that military strength was to be linked with any concept of national honor or progress. Again, the sun was used to symbolize power and energy. This time the image included a myriad of rays emanating from the sun that represented perhaps the far-reaching influence of the party.

The next postcard (page 61) conveys a similar sense of energy and progress. It also has extreme visual impact with its bold use of color. The card was issued to promote the East Prussian Sea Service. This service was created to facilitate transportation from the main part of Germany to East Prussia which was separated from the rest of Germany under the Treaty of Versailles. The content of this card is

Postcard featuring German work ethic: "Honor and Work." Artwork by United Art Institute, Kaulbeuren. *Author's Collection.*

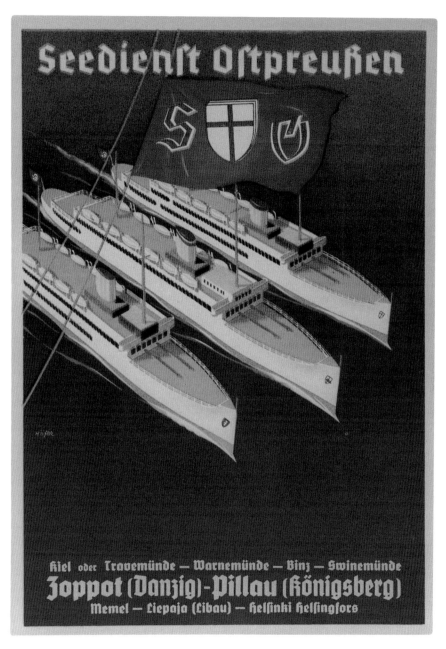

Postcard created for East Prussia Sea Service. Published by Seedienst Ostpreussen, Germany. *Author's Collection.*

certainly not intended to be overtly political. However, it would have served as a subtle reminder of the separation of East Prussia from Germany. It was this split that created the need for such a service in the first place. The card also serves as another example of the high level of sophistication Germany had achieved in its production of postal cards by the late 1930s. It is not dated but can be placed in the late 1930s because of the style of the ships and the fact that each flies a swastika flag. The card also seems to convey a feeling of energy and modernity characteristic of this period in German propaganda.

The next piece of postal propaganda will serve as a final illustration of the early days of Nazi rule. In some ways, it could be considered one of the most influential pieces of propaganda of this period. To better understand why, one must "revisit" the economic crisis that had been hammering away at German lives. By 1938, many Germans began to believe their financial situation was finally improving. Some economists of the day cited lowered expectations as an explanation of this somewhat flawed perception. Grunberger also observed this change in attitude. He writes, "By 1938 most people not only knew themselves to be far more affluent than in 1932, but also . . . thought themselves better off than before the Depression."[6]

This feeling of being "better off" helps to explain the propaganda appeal of the "Volkswagen" project. This program was promoted as a way for ordinary Germans to purchase their own automobile.[7] This would have been an impossible thought for ordinary citizens in most parts of the world in the late 1930s. Not only was much of the world still in depression, it was difficult to find financial institutions willing to lend money for the purchase of a car at the time. So, in order to ensure interest in this program, the National Socialist German government devised a payroll deduction scheme that made it possible for Germans to pay for their car in advance (prior to delivery of the car). This program was used to further promote Hitler's intended message that things were better now.

This clever use of propaganda succeeded as "thousands of Germans enthusiastically responded to the *Volkswagen* scheme."[8] The special cancellation shown here commemorates the groundbreaking ceremonies at the Volkswagen plant in Rothenfelde in 1938. Note the subtle use of the swastika (again seen in a representation of the sun) to remind the viewer of who was responsible for this symbol of national pride and prosperity. Unfortunately, for those Germans who chose to participate, the outbreak of the war in 1939 forced the Volkswagen plant to convert its production to strictly military purposes. Therefore, those who had

Postmark commemorating groundbreaking at the new Volkswagen factory, 1938. German postal authority. *Author's Collection.*

contributed toward the purchase of a new Volkswagen saw neither their cars nor their money again.[9]

These examples illustrate a pivotal stage in the evolution of propaganda in German postal materials. Beginning in 1933, postal materials were used to serve the political needs of the National Socialist Government by reflecting the images and impressions that the government wanted its citizens to receive. These desired images were used to convey a sense of smooth transition and, at the same time, a sense of progress and accomplishment. In addition, these postal materials illustrated the skillful development of printing and artistic capabilities associated with their publication. Thus, hand in hand, the message *and* messenger (the postal items) became a more sophisticated and more potent propaganda tool.

CHAPTER FIVE

Early Territorial Expansion: 1935-1939

In the eyes of the German people perhaps nothing demonstrated the "success" of Hitler's programs more than the expansion of German territory. From the plebiscite and reoccupation of the Saarland in 1934-35, Germans on average saw a major territorial expansion every two years. When one considers that all of these expansions (prior to 1939) were accomplished without firing a shot, one readily sees how these territorial acquisitions could be considered virtual miracles in the eyes of ordinary Germans. Of course, as one might expect, the postal record of these events shows a significant effort to milk them for their maximum propaganda value.

The first "maximum propaganda" opportunity came when the Germans annexed Austria on March 13, 1938. This event is frequently referred to as the Anschluss. In the early stages of the Anschluss, the postage stamps of Austria were still valid for a brief time. This led to "mixed frankings" of German and Austrian stamps. As this postcard shows (opposite top), it became quite popular to mail items with a stamp from each country. This example, postmarked August 15, 1938, has a German stamp on the left and an Austrian stamp on the right.

A related postal item is seen in the illustration below opposite. Here, one sees that the corner of a postcard carries a special slogan referring to the takeover. The cancellation urged the citizens to "vote yes" on the tenth of April to confirm the "Anschluss." (Here, only an Austrian stamp was used.)

Postcard back with German and Austrian postage stamps. German and Austrian postal authorities. *Author's Collection.*

Postage stamp with slogan urging voters to vote in favor of Austrian annexation. Austrian postal authority. *Author's Collection.*

Postcard commemorating Anschluss with map showing Austria as a part of Germany. Published by Brendamour, Simhart & Co., Munich. *Author's Collection.*

Numerous other postal items were created in an effort to gain as much recognition for this territorial accomplishment as possible. Shown opposite is a colorful example of an official card marking the Anschluss. For the first time, Germans were given a view of the new Germany that now included Austria within its borders. It bears the slogan: "One People, One Nation, One Leader." German Nazi propaganda had reached a new level of development. Subtlety was definitely gone. Hitler's image was no longer placed alongside a previous leader; now he *was* the leader.

The final item commemorating the Anschluss is a somewhat curious example illustrating the pressures to conform (below). Apparently, at the time of the unification, someone had a rather large stock of postcards already printed (or ready for printing) bearing a photograph of the Ring Strasse in Vienna, Austria. With careful examination, one can see that someone retouched the flags pictured flying alongside the street. The irregular and disproportionate size of the white circles within the flags shows that they have been retouched to now carry the swastika emblem. Presumably this was done because it would have been difficult, if not impossible, to sell or use postcards bearing the flag of the prior Austrian regime

Postcard with photograph of Nazi German flag in Vienna. Published by PAG. *Author's Collection.*

following the annexation. Had this not been altered, it is likely that it would not have passed the Nazi censorship.

This card demonstrates how quickly and easily the everyday aspects of society were manipulated to create the appearance of support and conformity to the new order under Nazism. This push toward conformity was quite consistent with one of Hitler's major goals. This was the goal of "Gleichschaltung" which is sometimes translated as the coordination of German society. David Schoenbaum explains this concept is his book entitled, *Hitler's Social Revolution*. He describes Gleichschaltung as "the pressure toward political monopoly before which all parties, all interest groups, fraternal organizations, church groups, and even Boy Scouts bowed."[1] It was this same pressure to conform that led the seller of the previously illustrated card to add the swastika image. In all likelihood, this did not require official intervention and was done voluntarily.

The next significant annexation of territory by Germany was the seizure of the Sudetenland. This event was perhaps the single most celebrated political event in Germany's entire postal history. Nearly every town within the so-called Sudetenland prepared its own special postal cancellations to mark the occasion. Overnight, the names of towns reverted to their former German (Austrian) names, and a plethora of commemorative postcards and other materials were prepared. While the Munich agreement was signed only on the 29th of September 1938, pivotal political events were quickly coming to a head. For example, in early September 1938, Hitler spoke at the Nazi party congress in Nuremberg (the Reichsparteitag). The theme of his speech was, quite predictably, the Sudetenland and Czechoslovakia. This speech, in turn, sparked a series of violent pro-German incidents in the Sudeten region.[2] Therefore, it is not surprising that as early as September 21 the city of As (Asch in German) declared itself independent. A commemorative cancellation and postcard were already prepared for the occasion. This item (opposite top), postmarked September 21, 1938, was cancelled more than a week *before* the Munich agreement was signed. This points to the tremendous upheaval that was present in the region even as the talks were underway. The stamp used was Czechoslovakian, and the printed slogan with Nazi eagle and swastika reads: "We have borne the yoke, now we are free and will remain free."

A special commemorative postcard was also issued that same day. On this rather well executed card (opposite below), the swastika was proudly displayed along with images of four individuals bearing arms with determined expressions on their faces. In the lower left corner, a map was included on which the Asch

Above: Czechoslovakian postage stamp with bilingual postmark and slogan. Czechoslovakian postal authority. *Author's Collection.*

Right: Nazi Sudeten propaganda postcard for Asch. Published by CK. *Author's Collection.*

Retouched photo postcard of Barzdorf. (No information about publisher or photographer appears on postcard.) *Author's Collection.*

Address side of Barzdorf postcard with propaganda cancellations. (No information about publisher or photographer appear on postcard.) *Author's Collection.*

region was highlighted. This map reveals the close proximity of this town to other Czech/Sudeten cities. This particular card is postmarked September 30. However, the card was actually released on September 21.[3] Therefore, the card must have been planned and created *weeks* before the finalization of the Munich agreement. This fact clearly demonstrates the high levels of anticipation and enthusiasm associated with this event.

The front and back of the next card (opposite) is perhaps even more interesting. The front side depicts the small town of Barzdorf in Eastern Sudetenland. Barzdorf was located near what was then the German town of Glatz in Silesia. Here, one sees evidence of another postcard being altered by someone. It appears that a pro-German took a tourist postcard that read "Barzdorf C.S.R." (Czechoslovak Republic) and drew a swastika over the "C. S. R." The card was mailed with Czech stamps and postmarked at two different locations. The bottom cancellation reveals another piece of postal propaganda as the swastika appeared in conjunction with the symbol of the Sudeten German Party.

This particular card was addressed to Grafenburg which, like Barzdorf, was located in Sudetenland. The city of Grafenburg was actually in an area of Sudetenland that would have required the card to have either been carried over German territory or over Czech territory for delivery. Since there was no "return to sender" legend on the card, it can be presumed that the card was actually delivered. Since the official transfer of the Sudetenland to German control did not occur until October 1, 1938, this postcard (with its September 1938 cancellation) provides more evidence of the enthusiastic support this takeover received *prior* to its actual occurrence!

Throughout the entire region the postal authorities in each community obviously had prepared well for this long anticipated event. These postal materials reveal how eagerly the citizens in these small towns awaited the coming of the Germans. The words of Siegfried Fischer (born in Sudetenland) shed some light on the feelings of many ethnic Germans concerning this historic event:

> With the beginning of the Third Reich we began to hope that our situation in the Sudetenland would improve. The German occupation in 1938 was not felt to be an occupation at all. Rather, we waited in happy anticipation for the German troops finally to liberate us. The soldiers were received with flowers and great hospitality.[4]

As the previous postcards attest, this "happy anticipation" was certainly felt by postal authorities in each community as they prepared an enormous volume of postal issues to commemorate this long awaited event. As the next card illustrates (below), many of these "commemorative" items were also quite elaborate. This card was postmarked in Burgstein on Oct 12, 1938. The cancellation in the upper left reads: "Adolf Hitler has liberated us!" A second cancellation, placed under the stamps, reads: "Sudetenland returns home to the Reich!" The card itself features a photo of the town of Burgstein along with a swastika and symbol of the Sudeten German Party. Again, the sender placed a Czech stamp (overprinted with a swastika) alongside the German stamp. This postcard represents one of the most elaborate and carefully prepared Sudeten postal items from this era. The fact that such a sophisticated card originated from Burgstein seems especially remarkable since it was such a small town. The population in 1938 was less than 2,000.[5]

The final example of postal materials created to celebrate the Munich Agreement was actually privately prepared. The postcard shown opposite (postmarked on October 9, 1939) was posted with stamps from both Czechoslovakia and Germany and includes a very exuberant message. It reads: "One People! One

Postcard with German and overprinted Czechoslovakian postage stamps from the village of Burgstein. (No information about publisher or photographer appears on postcard.) *Author's Collection.*

Privately produced postcard with Czechoslovakian and German postage stamps, October 1938. Czechoslovakian and German postal authorities. *Author's Collection.*

Nation! One Leader! Thanks to the Liberator!" Again, one sees the unrestrained enthusiasm that characterized the response to this historic event, at least on the part of the ethnic Germans.

Whether privately prepared or officially sanctioned, the postal materials created to commemorate and celebrate the Munich Agreement displayed an eagerness for the control of Sudetenland to change to German hands. The postcards and stamps also revealed a ready willingness to proclaim the new German names of the towns. While the transfer of power to Germany took place on October 1, 1938, many of the postal items proclaimed a "day of liberation" after that date. It would appear that the later postal materials were prepared to commemorate the actual arrival of German troops or other authorities to their cities or towns. Others items may have been prepared after the transfer of the postal apparatus to the new regime. In most cases, however, it is apparent that a measure of advanced preparation was necessary to produce the kind of elaborate material that was available *very* early after the transfer of power from the Czech to the German government.

As was the situation with Austria, the Sudeten residents were provided with an opportunity to ratify their annexation with a plebiscite. Naturally, this too, called for the use of propaganda, including postal propaganda, to promote this important vote which was held on Dec 12, 1938. These cards were prepared as part of postal propaganda efforts to encourage citizens to vote for the annexation. The first postcard (below) was cancelled in Znaim on Dec 4, 1938. The message on the cancellation reads: "For the Fuhrer a Yes." The second card (opposite) was posted in Troppau on Dec 4, 1938. Its cancellation message was in two parts: "In Liberated Sudetenland" and "Election and Confession (or declaration of faith) Day." Yet the most interesting aspect of this card is found in the handwritten message. It translates: "Heil Hitler! We have succeeded!" A final point of interest found in these cards is seen in the stamps used. By December of 1938, regular German stamps were now in use. In the previous months, Czech, or Czech and German, combinations were still permitted.

The subject of the Sudetenland is significant, not only in the study of history, but also in the study of the development of postal propaganda. By examining these postal materials, a student of history can see tangible documentation of the Nazi regime expanding into new territory. Examination of the postal materials also suggests that the response to this expansion was significantly different than what

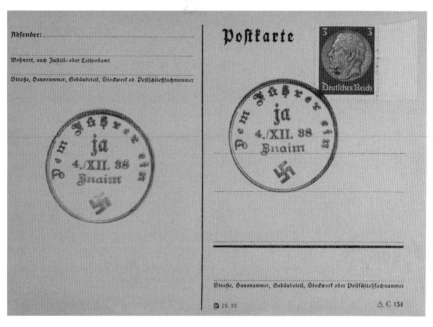

Postcard with German postage stamp and postmark urging people to vote in favor of the annexation of Sudetenland. German postal authority. *Author's Collection.*

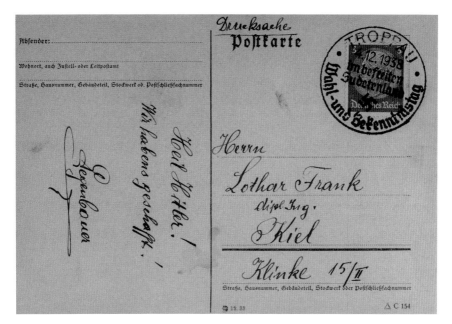

Postcard with German postage stamp and special postmark for Sudeten plebiscite. Official German postal authority. *Author's Collection.*

one might have expected. As the swastika cast its shadow across the Sudetenland, the postal materials confirm that there was a substantial measure of eagerness for the German takeover. It was, in fact, viewed by many as a "liberation" rather than an annexation. While there no doubt were dissenters, it is clear that there was a widespread, spontaneous and enthusiastic reception for the new order.

This enthusiasm cannot be explained merely by the official control that was so much in evidence in Nazi Germany at the time. Instead, as the postal materials reveal, these were largely a people who seemed to welcome the prospect of becoming a part of the Reich in the autumn months of 1938. These were also a people, however, who had been very cleverly manipulated by propaganda for many years. This continual daily conditioning (even in their reading of the mail each day) must certainly have helped shape their views to support the takeover. Furthermore, both these "new" Germans *and* most Germans appeared not only to support the takeover, but seemed to genuinely support Hitler, himself. This feeling is summed up quite well in the words of Richard Bessel in his book, *Life in the Third Reich*. Bessel writes:

Hitler's imposing series of 'triumphs without bloodshed' directed at 'peace with honour' — tearing up the Versailles settlement, winning back the Saar, restoring 'military sovereignty,' recovering the Rhineland, uniting Austria with Germany, and bringing the Sudetenland 'home into the Reich' — won him support in all sections of the German people and unparalleled popularity, prestige and acclaim.[6]

CHAPTER SIX

The Nazi Cult and the Racial State

Pseudo-religion

A particularly curious phenomenon of Nazi Germany was the use of propaganda to bring about the creation of an almost quasi-religious cult of Nazi culture. This began with Hitler's creation of numerous "holidays" throughout the German year. Among these newly established holidays were the January 30th "Assumption of Power" holiday, the April 20th "Birthday of Adolf Hitler" holiday, the May 1st "Day of German Labor" holiday (previously May Day), the annual Reichsparteitag, or Party Congress, held in Nuremberg each September, and the Harvest Festival celebrated in Bueckeberg each October.[1] Another new annual commemoration was the November 5th "Beer Hall Putsch" holiday. On this date each year, Hitler led a solemn procession of the putsch survivors through the streets of Munich and then laid wreaths upon the graves of those Nazis who had fallen on that day in 1923.[2] Such observances had great appeal to the emotions. This was no coincidence for Hitler believed that "propaganda must be addressed to the emotions and not to the intelligence."[3]

Of course, as with much of the Nazis' plans to consolidate power, these commemorations were phased in slowly, yet deliberately. Year after year, Germans saw new holidays established and old holidays "re-christened" as the Nazi party strove to gain the people's reverence. In the book, *The 12-Year Reich*, Richard Grunberger examined this Nazi move toward "pseudo-religion." He writes: "A key device for inculcating this mood of reverence was the institution of a cycle of high holy days that leavened the mundane routine of the year with uplifting occasions. In this way, a sequence of Nazi red-letter days . . . was evolved."[4]

Research indicates only one example of a postal item honoring the "holiday" of Hitler's birthday in 1936. It was a postcard issued by the German Civil Servants Association and was sold to raise funds for the Olympic games of 1936. Although this card was promoted as an Adolf Hitler "birthday donation," it did not even show a picture of Hitler on it.[5]

The following year, however, a postal souvenir sheet was created for this occasion. This rather elaborate and dramatic issue marks another major development in postal propaganda (below). For the first time, Hitler's portrait appeared on an official German postage stamp. The inscription underneath the stamps reads: "He who would rescue a people, knows only heroic thoughts."

The issuance of this souvenir sheet began an annual postal commemoration of Hitler's birthday. These birthday celebrations also became occasions for the propaganda apparatus to portray a soft and kind image of Hitler as can be seen in the following postcard (opposite). This card was part of an official series issued in 1939 as part of Hitler's 50th birthday celebration. It portrays a group of children presenting birthday gifts of flowers to Hitler while giving the symbolic straight-armed salute. The smiling "Fuehrer" is shown accepting a bouquet from the youngest

Envelope with Hitler souvenir sheet of postage stamps on front. German postal authority. *Author's Collection.*

78

Postcard with photograph of Hitler receiving birthday greetings from a group of children. German postal authority. *Author's Collection.*

of the children. (Note the new use of "decorative" swastikas along the border of the card.)

As with the images of progress and accomplishment seen earlier in this study, the type of postal propaganda seen on this card also served the regime well as they continued their campaign to shape public opinion. Clearly, this card was created with the goal of convincing Germans that Hitler was a kind, fatherly figure and a benevolent leader. Another interesting aspect of this card is that it is very possible that the photo used on it was taken by Hitler's female companion, Eva Braun.[6]

Not only were postal materials created to celebrate Hitler's quasi-religious holidays, postal items were also created to portray the words and deeds of Hitler in an almost religious manner. The following two postcards are prime examples of this genre in propaganda. The first card (shown on page 80), mailed in February 1940, is a reproduction of a propaganda artwork showing the young Hitler speaking before a crowd of early supporters. The "Biblical" message along the bottom is particularly startling. It reads: "In the Beginning was the Word." Note the dramatic use of lighting in the scene and the hypnotic effect Hitler's words seemed to have on his listeners. There is little doubt that this postal item was designed to establish a connection in people's minds between Hitler and God. In fact, it does not require much imagination at all to draw a correlation between this image and that of Jesus with the disciples in the famous *Last Supper* painting by Leonardo DaVinci.

The next postcard (opposite) further illustrates postal propaganda's religious bent. Here, one sees a different style of postcard. No photograph or illustration appears. Instead, the words of Hitler are conveyed in a manner similar to that found in ancient religious manuscripts. The message, too, is of an almost "scriptural" nature. The words translate roughly: "If the German people themselves place their trust in me, I will become their courageous and loyal champion."

At this point, one suspects that some Germans who were familiar with religious texts and traditions would have viewed such materials as sacrilegious. Yet, for many Germans, particularly those caught up in the ecstatic cult of "Fuehrer worship," the parallels to Christian religious methods and teaching must have seemed altogether appropriate.

To better understand this notion of Germans viewing Hitler as a religious figure, one might refer to the lyrics sung by the Hitler Youth at the 1934 Nuremberg Rally. The children sang: "No evil priest can prevent us from feeling that we are

„Am Anfang war das Wort"

Postcard with artwork portraying an Hitler speech in the early days. Published by Verlag Franz Hanfstaengl, Munich. *Author's Collection.*

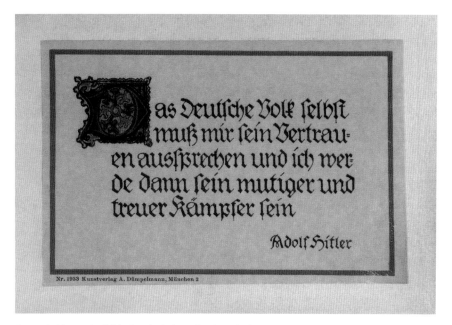

Postcard with words of Hitler in style similar to illuminated religious manuscript. Published by U. Dumpelmann, Munich. *Author's Collection.*

the children of Hitler. We follow not Christ, but Horst Wessel. Away with incense and holy water. The Church can go hang for all we care. The Swastika brings salvation on earth."[7] These lyrics not only point to the fact that many German people were accepting Hitler as a religious figure, they were also simultaneously rejecting aspects of the established religious traditions. Young people, in particular, were being indoctrinated into this cult.

The adulation and deification of Hitler may have reached its "postal pinnacle" in 1941. The next two stamps (page 82) reveal that in this year the portrait of Hitler finally replaced that of Hindenburg on regular issue postage stamps. The significance of this event may not have even been noticed at first by the average German citizen. This was because one would probably have to look twice to even notice much difference between the two stamps. It was certainly no accident that the new Hitler stamps were produced in the same size, in the same color and even in the same "12 pfennig" denomination as the Hindenburg stamps had been. In fact these color and denomination parallels with the Hindenburg stamps were found in all of the various denominations of this series of stamps.

With this technique two things were accomplished. First, this tactic allowed the transition to the Hitler image to be smooth and subtle. Secondly, it encouraged

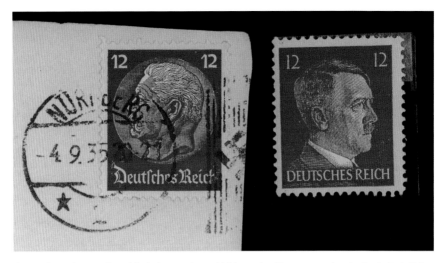

Comparison of stamps from Hindenburg series and Hitler series. German postal authority. *Author's Collection.*

the minds of the viewer to draw a parallel (perhaps unconsciously) between Hitler and the enormously popular statesman and military hero, Hindenburg. It is very likely that such tremendous efforts were expended in the planning of even the minor details of the regime's postage stamps. These seemingly little decisions must have been especially important during the war year of 1941.

Racist Propaganda

Another central element of Nazi postal propaganda, if not *the* central element, is the concept of German racial superiority. This premise is most commonly thought of in terms of its most basic manifestation: Nazi German anti-Semitism. Yet, it is important to remember that anti-Semitism was not an unfamiliar concept to Germans long before the rise of Hitler. This fact is supported in Daniel Goldhagen's book, *Hitler's Willing Executioners.* In writing this book, Goldhagen extensively researched the roots of anti-Semitism in German culture. He writes:

> From the beginning of the nineteenth century, anti-Semitism was ubiquitous in Germany. . . . Jews came to be identified with and symbolic of anything and everything which was deemed awry in German society. . . . The cognitive model of Nazi anti-Semitism had taken shape well before the Nazis came to power.[8]

This attitude was also evidenced in the postal arena. In fact, there are examples of postcards from as early as the 19th century portraying Jews as objects of hatred and ridicule. Even during the 1920s, when Germany's currency crisis was rampant and individual towns and jurisdictions were forced to create their own paper money, a few smaller communities created anti-Jewish images for use on their local currency. This must have served as an assertion that Jews were somehow "responsible" for the economic misfortune of Germans.

Yet, all in all, the occurrence of such blatant racism was still somewhat rare. While anti-Semitic propaganda gained more widespread use under Hitler, particularly as an expression of "official" opinion, there were still not large numbers of examples of deliberately racist postal items in circulation during the Nazi regime. A few notorious examples that do exist include the promotional postcards issued to advertise the "Eternal Jew Exposition." This was a Nazi sponsored event designed to demonstrate to the public at large the Party's position with regard to Jews and to encourage public animosity toward them. While the event was held in various locations throughout Germany, the card illustrated on page 84 was prepared to promote the show held in Vienna in August of 1938. The image portrays a stereotypical Eastern European Jew with a map of either Germany or the Soviet Union under one arm. The Soviet "hammer and sickle" symbol was even superimposed on the map. In one hand he holds what appears to be a whip or a riding crop, and his other hand is filled with coins. This was an obvious reference to the "money grubber" image the Nazis liked to attribute to Jews.[9]

At this stage in Hitler's rise to power, the Nazi Party pursued a new path in its propaganda campaign as they sought to convey negative images of Jews. Now, they attempted to portray Judaism and Communism as somehow equal in the eyes of the public. Anti-Semitic films such as the notorious "Jud Suss" were produced as one method to indoctrinate the public into this way of thinking. At the same time, propaganda referring to the "Jewish Bolshevik Conspiracy" was becoming more commonplace, especially after the invasion of the Soviet Union. One aspect of this misinformation campaign was to "prove" that the common citizens of the Soviet Union were forced to live in inhuman conditions due to the failures of their system of government. This, in turn, planted the seed for a correlation to be drawn: if the people of the Soviet Union lived like animals, they must truly be the "subhumans" that Nazi racial ideology taught. After all, how else would "subhumans" live than in "subhuman" conditions?

Propaganda postcard to publicize the "Eternal Jew" exhibition in Vienna, 1938. *Reprinted by permission of R. James Bender Publishing.*

Once again, the Nazi Government created a traveling exhibition to spread its message. This exhibit was entitled the "Soviet Paradise Exhibition." Its purpose was to give the German people examples of how "ordinary" people lived inside the Soviet Union.[10] The exhibit included displays of "everyday Soviet life" supposedly documented by German troops as they advanced into Soviet territory. The postcard at the top of page 86 was designed to highlight the upcoming exhibit in Berlin with a photograph showing a reconstruction of a "typical" Soviet home. The card was actually postmarked at the exhibit that took place between May 2nd and June 21st in 1942. Even the exhibition's closing date was another sign of the Nazi party's attention to detail. June 21st was the first anniversary of the German invasion of the Soviet Union. The reverse side of the postcard is seen at the bottom of page 86. The caption on the upper left side reads: "Hovel of a cab driver and his wife outside of a major city in the paradise of the worker and peasant." Part of the wording used in this caption was taken from Soviet propaganda of the time. The USSR was sometimes referred to as a paradise of worker and peasant. Even the postmark was intended to influence thinking. It shows a mother with her starving child and the sad face of what appears to be an industrial or mining worker. This same postmark image appeared on posters advertising the exhibit.

One unanticipated result of the exhibit was an attempt by the Baum group (a young group of anti-Nazis) to burn down the Berlin exhibit. This group's unsuccessful attempt to shut down the exhibit resulted in the arrests and murders of over five hundred Berlin Jews in reprisal. Death sentences were handed down to nine of twelve convicted conspirators.[11]

It is no wonder that the Baum group was upset with this propaganda. The exhibit was undoubtedly quite successful in reinforcing the message that the "subhumans" who lived within the Soviet Union were indeed animals. Although this propaganda might have seemed a bit incredible to the observer, the sentiment behind these amazing images was often echoed by the letters being sent home from soldiers on the eastern front. One soldier writing to his mother in 1941 had this to say about the Soviet Union:

> These people here . . . live like animals. If they could only once see a German living room. That would be paradise for them, a paradise that these communist scoundrels, Jews and criminals have denied them. We have seen the true face of Bolshevism, have gotten to know it and experienced it, and will know how to deal with it in the future.[12]

Right: Postcard to promote the "Soviet Paradise" exhibition in Berlin, 1942. (No information about publisher or photograph appears on postcard.) *Author's Collection.*

Below: Stamp side of "Soviet Paradise" exhibition postcard with special postmark commemorating exhibit. German postal authority. *Author's Collection.*

AUSSTELLUNG »DAS SOWJET-PARADIES«
BERLIN, LUSTGARTEN. 9. MAI BIS 21. JUNI 1942

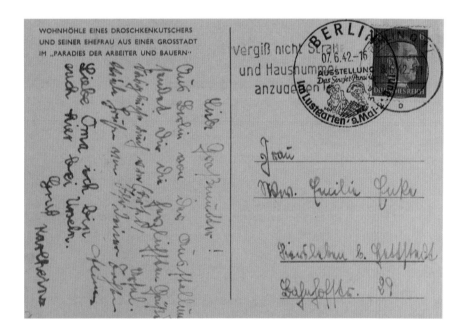

Another soldier sent home a similar message that same year: "It is, I believe, the most depraved and filthiest [people] living on God's earth. Hardly ever do you see the face of a person who seems rational and intelligent. . . . The wild, half-crazy look in their eyes makes them appear like imbeciles."[13] While the overt racism of such material may have been somewhat infrequent, the Nazis still created more of such material than was common to earlier periods of German history.

More commonly, the racist message on postal material of the day took a different approach. Usually, the Nazi party sought to promote the "positive" by creating a flood of Aryan racial images. This was probably done to establish a clear contrast between the "subhuman" images and that of the "ideal" citizens. Below, one sees several postage stamps from this time period. German mailboxes were flooded with these stamps, and each was designed to illustrate the ideal Aryan or German. It is ironic that Germans of that period failed to realize that many, if not most, of the highest ranking German leaders, such as Hitler, Goering, or Goebbels, failed to live up to this supposed physical and racial ideal.

Five postage stamps displaying "ideal Aryan" types. German postal authority. *Author's Collection.*

However, in this study of German racial policy, the most frightening and graphic examples were found in another facet of postal materials. These propagandist items represented the extreme Nazi law that dealt with the identification of all German Jews. Jewish social isolation was given its clearest expression in the ordinance that went into effect on January 1, 1939: All Jews were required to add the name 'Israel' (for males) or 'Sara' (for females) to their first names if their own names did not appear in a special official list of 'typically Jewish' names issued by the interior minister.[14] This marked a major step in the control and monitoring of the Jewish people and the eventual gathering up of Jews for concentration camps.

The postal item shown below demonstrates this practice. This letter was mailed from Dresden by "Max 'Israel' Steinhart" in December 1940. It was sent to "Gerhard and Erwin Steinhart" who were apparently being held at a civilian internment camp in Canada. The markings indicate that the letter had been read by both a German censor (as it left Germany) and a Canadian censor (upon its arrival in Canada). This letter is particularly extraordinary because of the time in which it was mailed. The postmark was just weeks before all able bodied Jews were conscripted into forced labor.[15] At the time this letter was written, Jews had already been placed into

Censored envelope showing the required Jewish identification information. Private correspondence. *Author's Collection.*

the highest possible tax bracket regardless of income and were being charged an additional 15% "social compensation tax."[16] It was in September 1941 that all Jews were required to wear the yellow Star of David for identification purposes.[17]

By this time, it is apparent that Adolf Hitler had made great strides in promoting his agenda. Not only were the German people looking to him as their leader of an almost "religious" movement, but his agenda for "inferior" races was also taking hold. All these things were accomplished, at least in part, through the extensive use of propaganda. The postal materials examined in this chapter were just a few of the hundreds of similar items prepared during this period. One can only imagine how powerful the effects of this "poisonous" material must have been as Germans received a dose of it in their mail each and every day.

CHAPTER SEVEN

The War and Its Postal Manifestations

A s might be expected, the outbreak of the war in September of 1939 was well documented throughout Germany on its postal material. Not only were stamps and postcards used to glorify the German military's territorial expansion, but they were also useful in making a case for the war in the first place. "Though propaganda has never been a substitute for military strength, extensive resources or skillful negotiation, it has often played an important role in wartime strategy."[1]

One such "strategy" is seen in the postcard shown opposite. It was designed to portray Poland as a threat to German security by contrasting the aggressive Polish troop positions with those of Germany. The message along the top reads: "Who Needs Security in the East?" This implied that the threatening placement of troops along the German-Polish border placed Poland in a much stronger position than Germany and that concerns about Germany's policies were misplaced. Although there is no date on the card, it was presumably prepared to influence public opinion in favor of military preparation against Poland.

This is a very revealing example of the type of propaganda seen inside the Third Reich with regard to the coming war. Today in the West, there is often a tendency to view the outbreak of war against Poland as a clear-cut case of aggression. Germans of the time were taught differently. The book, *Voices From the Third Reich*, written by Steinhoff, Pechel and Showalter, can help one better understand

Propaganda postcard showing Polish and German troop positions on map. Published by Verlag Deutscher Lichtbilddienst, Berlin. *Author's Collection.*

this German viewpoint. Here is an excerpt from an interview with Jutta Rudiger, a German woman who had met Hitler on two occasions. Jutta describes the pro war propaganda she recalled:

> We had reports of how Germans in Poland were being persecuted, and how the Poles were saying, 'On to Berlin!' We were told Hitler's first demands were moderate, that he only wanted the Polish Corridor. There was even a joke about Hitler telling a Polish countess: 'Madame, I don't want your whole castle; I'll be satisfied with the corridor.'[2]

Historians might also point to the phony radio station attack at Gleiwitz as another example of propaganda staged for public consumption to further generate pro war sentiment within Germany. It seems clear that there was an elaborate, multi-faceted, long-term propaganda effort designed to justify *and* generate public support for action against Poland. William Sheridan Allen examined such phenomena in his book, *The Nazi Seizure of Power*. Allen extensively researched the Nazi influence in one small German town which he referred to as "Thalburg." He writes: "Thus in the. . . Nazi regime, Thalburg was subjected to a veritable barrage of propaganda. . . . The total effect was to create the spirit of a revolution and to justify the kinds of steps the Nazis took to insure themselves control over the people."[3] It is fascinating to note how this attempt to justify action against a strong, aggressive Poland, may have inadvertently conveyed an image of an unprepared and rather weak Germany.

However, much more common wartime images found in this "barrage of propaganda" portrayed the German military as strong, energetic, heroic and efficient. The postcards on pages 93-94 illustrate this concept well. The first postcard comes from a series entitled: "Our Waffen-SS." The second card also comes from a series called: "The Freedom Struggle of Greater Germany for a New Europe." Both are pieces of propaganda that were designed to display hardworking soldiers using powerful and advanced equipment. These cards became favorite collectibles and served the purpose of showing support for the military while providing the public with an officially sanctioned image of military life and exploits.

The regime also encouraged the public's fascination with the military by issuing several series of postage stamps. The twelve stamps shown on page 95 (printed in a 1943 series) featured images of various weapons in action. It appears that the artist took great care to show a sense of movement and power. One is particularly

Postcard with photograph of Waffen-SS soldier. Published by Kunstverlag, E.A. Schwerdtfeger, Berlin. Photo by S.S. Kriegsberichter Roth. *Author's Collection.*

Postcard with color photograph of U-boat crew. Published by Verlag Franz Zabel, Dessau. *Author's Collection.*

struck by the image of the Stukas on the "25 pfennig" denomination and the SS insignia on the soldiers who appear on the "4 pfennig" denomination. These scenes undoubtedly struck terror in the hearts of millions of Europeans during the war. Yet, to ordinary Germans, these images were designed to convey a sense of strength and invulnerability.

Twelve postage stamps portraying various German military units. German postal authority. *Author's Collection.*

Privately produced postcard with photograph of group of soldiers. Photograph by Photo-Haus Drogerie Schafer. *Author's Collection.*

Privately produced postcard with photograph of soldiers marching. Photograph by Foto-Pohle, Konigsberg (PR). *Author's Collection.*

The postal authorities issued a similar set of twelve stamps one year later. However, on the 1944 issues, the name "Deutsches Reich" had become "Grossdeutsches Reich" or Greater Germany. This term came to be used on nearly all postage stamps and postal material created after the latter part of 1943. This subtle change signified the tremendous expansion of German territory into newly occupied areas of Europe. Ironically, the term did not enjoy widespread general use until the borders of that "Greater Germany" were already beginning to experience a dramatic contraction.

World War Two postal materials also shared parallels with some of the traditions of World War One. One of these was the affinity for a soldier's particular military unit. Often, private photo cards were issued for each soldier to show himself in the midst of his military comrades. The two cards on the opposite page illustrate this practice. Both are actual photographs that were made into postcards. The backs of each card were prepared to allow for them to be mailed. Careful inspection of the bottom card reveals a cross marked above one individual in the center of the postcard. This may have been done by the original owner of the card to point to his own image or perhaps that of a comrade who became an early casualty of the war. Both cards reflect the spirit of unity that was such a key part of a soldier's survival. The words of Guy Sajer in *The Forgotten Soldier* sum up this feeling:

Tapfere kleine Soldatenfrau
Lied von Carl Sträßer

1. Als wir im August hinausgezogen sind, / Da hast du mich zum Sammelplatz gebracht. / Du trugst auf deinem Arm unser kleinstes Kind, / Und du hast mich so fröhlich angelacht. / Du sagtest unserem Jungen: „Schau, dort steht der Vater ja!" / Und du warst eine kleine tapfere Frau, / Die ihren Liebsten scheiden sah.

1.—4. Tapfere kleine Soldatenfrau, / Warte nur bald, / Kehren wir zurück. / Tapfere kleine Soldatenfrau, / Du bist ja mein ganzes Glück / Tapfere kleine Soldatenfrau / Ich weiß wie so treu du denkst an mich. / Und so soll es immer sein, / Und so denk ich ja auch dein / Und aus dem Felde von Herzen grüß ich dich.

2. Als Abschied ich nahm, da war der Garten bunt, / Viel Rosen waren ringsumher erblüht. / Du gabst mir einen Kuß und dein roter Mund, / Der hat auch wie ein Röselein geglüht / Du drücktest mir die Hand so fest, / Da hab' ich's tief gespürt. / Daß mit Stolz in den Kampf du mich ziehen läßt, / Den Freiheitskampf, den Deutschland führt

3. Heut' bin ich so fern von dir und unserem Haus, / Doch fühl ich deine Grüße mit mir gehn / Ich rechne mir den Tag bis zum Urlaub aus, / Werd' dann dich und die Kinder wiedersehn. / Du stehst am Gartentore dann; / Wie schön ist da die Welt, / Wenn die tapfere Frau ihren feldgrauen Mann / In ihren Armen selig hält.

(wenden!)

Postcard of a soldier's farewell with lyrics of a song. Published by Spezial-Verlag, Robert Franke, Hamburg. Song by Musikverlags Eduard Alert, Berlin. *Author's Collection.*

Here, deep in the wilds of the steppe, we shall be all the more aware of our unity. We are surrounded by hatred and death . . . . Our group must be as one, and our thoughts must be identical. Your duty lies in your efforts to achieve that goal, and if we do achieve it, and maintain it, we shall be victors even in death.[4]

One can find another interesting characteristic that a few postal materials of this war shared with World War One: sentimentality. The postcard on page 97 illustrates this somewhat less common theme of German World War Two propaganda. It also displays the words to a song from the era entitled: "Brave Little Soldier's Wife," along with the image of a soldier on a troop train bidding farewell to his wife and child. While such sentimental cards existed during World War Two, research reveals nothing close to the tremendous volume that existed in World War One. If there was any propaganda intent in this card, it might be found in the expensive looking coat worn by the woman in the photo. In light of the deprivation normally experienced in wartime, one might conclude that these were rather wealthy people who chose to serve their country through military service. Another message that could be taken from the woman's attire was that Germany was not suffering

Postcard from a series of artcards of the Eastern Front. Published by Propaganda-Kompanie der Armee Busch. Artwork by Georg Vorhauer. *Author's Collection.*

Eastern Front feldpost artcard for Todt Organization. Published by O.T. Schulungsdienst. Artwork by Schidlewski. *Author's Collection.*

from the material deprivation usually associated with war. To the very end of the war Germany would continue to produce and distribute thousands of military images on stamps and postcards. But these glorified, and sometimes sentimental, images from early on eventually gave way to something quite different.

As the war in the east progressed, "propaganda company" (PK) artists produced surprisingly depressing images of the war in the Soviet Union. The card shown at th bottom of page 98 is from a set of fourteen color "artcards" printed in 1942 to illustrate the winter war on the eastern front. These artcards were done by soldier artists assigned to chronicle the war through their art. Here one sees the work of Georg Vorhauer, a war artist who was assigned to Russia and Italy. The significance of these artists' works was described by one German war artist, Heinz Hindorf, in the book, *German War Art 1939-1945*. Hindorf stated, "It must be acknowledged that all war artists knew the desire of the regime for glorification of its deeds . . . . Every war artist had to achieve a specific goal, even though not set out in detail, in order to retain his position."[5] Although this set of postcards was released for public consumption, the majority of work by these artists was intended to be exhibited after the German victory as a permanent record of the Third Reich's accomplishments. While perhaps not specifically intended as propaganda for the war, such cards must have influenced public opinion of the war by those who received them. This card certainly painted a rather depressing and forlorn picture of military life in Russia.

A second, similar card shown on page 99 displays the work of another war artist and is also dated 1942. This card was provided by the Todt Organization for use by soldiers on "feldpost" correspondence to the home front. As such, it is a bit shocking that such a forlorn and downbeat image was selected for use. Here is shown the bleakness of the Russian winters as a lone sentry guards what appears to be a mining facility. The scene depicted on this card is reminiscent of the words of one soldier in the book, *Frontsoldaten* by Stephen Fritz. The soldier described his experience in Russia: "The character of this landscape. . . was the highest stage of loneliness."[6] Indeed, such a sentiment comes through clearly when looking at this image.

One has to wonder why a government group such as the Todt Organization would sanction the use of a card that conveys such a sense of despair. One might have expected a much more glorified portrayal of the military situation at that time, particularly for the consumption of the "home front." One possible reason such cards were allowed to circulate was to create respect for the German solider. These postcards emphasized the sacrifices being made by these men. Yet, clearly, the primary intent of propaganda at this stage, no doubt, still remained: to *glorify* the military and justify Germany's military efforts.

CHAPTER EIGHT

The Conquest of New Territory

O ne of the most interesting aspects of German postal history during the course of the war is how the student and historian can quite literally follow the advance of German troops and the conquest of new territory through the study of stamps and other postal materials. As was seen in the case of the Sudetenland, Germans seemed almost obsessive in their desire to commemorate their territorial gains through postal means. In fact, it can be concluded that this was one of the most powerful forms of World War Two postal propaganda. Germany was very thorough in making sure that as territory was claimed, town names were immediately restored to their original pre-World War One German or Austrian names.

As seen with the Sudeten territories, the advance of German troops into Poland was accompanied by the rapid creation of makeshift postal materials to celebrate the return of these towns to German control. One of the earliest examples found demonstrating this propaganda is this postal cover from the town of Birnbaum (page 102, top). Prior to the war, this town was known by its Polish name of Miedzychod. The stamp used on this cover was from a set issued in October 1939. Note the rather crudely designed pear tree with a separate ink stamp bearing the name of the town. (The pear tree appears because "Birnbaum" is the German word for pear tree.) The card bears no message on the reverse and was likely sent to a stamp collector. Often, advancing troops would send home such items to their

Postcard with pear tree postmark, Birnbaum, 1939. German postal authority. *Author's Collection.*

Postmark of Posen (Polish Poznan), 1940. German postal authority. *Author's Collection.*

families and to stamp collector friends who wished to have unique items in their collections. This town eventually became part of a relatively vast area of Poland that was incorporated into the Reich rather than being considered an "occupied" Polish area.

Another much larger city that fell into this category was the city of Posen or "Poznan." This had been a major city of the pre-World War One German East with a population of between 250,000 and 300,000 in 1939.[1] It was also the birthplace of von Hindenburg. Here, one sees a portion of a postcard that was postmarked to commemorate the first anniversary of the city's return to Germany (opposite, below). The cancellation from October 1940 reads: "Wartheland Day of Liberation." The parts of Poland that were actually incorporated into the Reich either became part of East Prussia, West Prussia, Silesia or the new province of Wartheland.

Millions of ethnic Poles were later removed from places such as Birnbaum and Posen and moved into the "Polish" designated area called the Government General.[2] Here, too, beginning in 1940, Germany began producing special postal materials. Initially, these were Polish stamps overprinted with German symbols or propaganda slogans. Later, special stamps were created bearing the name of the Government General (shown below). Similarly, Germany had already created a

Postage stamps of occupied Poland and Bohemia/Moravia (Czechoslovakia). German postal authority. *Author's Collection.*

separate series of stamps for the occupied areas of Czechoslovakia called the Protectorate of Bohemia and Moravia. Several examples of these Polish and Bohemia/Moravia stamps are seen here. The first group consists of issues from the "Government General." Next are issues from the "Protectorate of Bohemia and Moravia." Notice the strong use of propaganda and German symbolism. The black stamp on the small white card is particularly noteworthy. It was issued as a memorial to Reinhard Heydrich, a favorite of SS leader, Heinrich Himmler. Heydrich was appointed "Reich Protector of Bohemia and Moravia" in 1941 and was assassinated in June of 1942. This stamp bears an image of Heydrich's death mask accompanied by the notorious SS runes.

Germany's obsession with postal propaganda is illustrated by the creation of this stamp. Although it was issued in 1943 to commemorate the first anniversary of Heydrich's death, a special printing of the already designed stamp was actually passed out in the form of a miniature sheet to a few dignitaries and honored guests at Heydrich's funeral. Today, these rare miniature sheets are highly prized by postal historians and are valued in the tens of thousands of dollars.

Another noteworthy aspect of the previous stamp relates to the career of Reinhard Heydrich. His administration of Czechoslovakia controlled the deportation and murder of Czech Jews. This included the administration of the camp systems. One camp under his control was that of Theresienstadt. From this camp, tens of thousands were ultimately sent to the death camps.[3] On the opposite page, one sees the front and back of a 1944 postcard acknowledging receipt of a parcel by an inmate at the Theresienstadt camp. This camp was sometimes referred to as the "model camp." SS overseers, such as Heydrich, decided that Theresienstadt could serve as a "model" which the Red Cross and other outside observers would be allowed to visit.[4] Inmates were instructed on proper behavior on those occasions when visitors were present. Since Theresienstadt was used primarily as a transit point en route to the death camps, care was taken to make sure visitors would observe only inmates who had recently arrived. In this way, visitors would believe that the inmates were well fed and healthy.

Much attention was paid to the camp's postal system which, at one point, even issued its own stamps. Parcel acknowledgment cards such as the one seen here were a part of this charade to create the appearance of normalcy and good treatment. Note that the message on the card was largely pre-printed so that the inmate was given no opportunity to add additional comments or pass along coded messages.

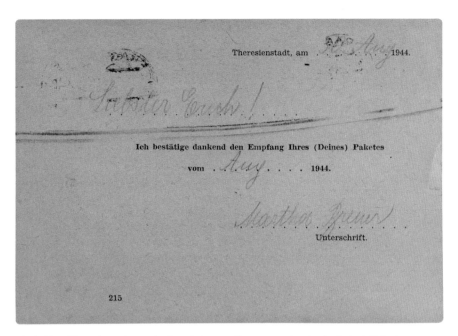

Back side of Theresienstadt parcel acknowledgment. German postal authority. *Author's Collection.*

Front side of Theresienstadt parcel acknowledgment card with Hitler stamps for Bohemia/Moravia. German postal authority. *Author's Collection.*

This represents a particularly sinister chapter in German wartime propaganda. It seems exceptionally disturbing that such elaborate schemes were contrived, including the manipulation of postal items, in an effort to misinform the public. These various attempts to fool people into believing all was well for Jewish residents assigned to the Theresienstadt camp revealed how far Hitler was willing to go in the war's propaganda effort. At the same time, it illustrates the careful planning and attention to detail that was an essential part of the "final solution!"

As German armies marched across Western Europe, they were almost always accompanied by postal materials "commemorating" these conquests. The German occupation of France and the low countries resulted in relatively little change in the postal status of those nations. France, Belgium, Netherlands, Denmark and Norway continued to issue stamps under the names of those countries. While the theme and content of such issues were no doubt closely controlled, little significant change was immediately apparent. However, Luxembourg, Alsace-Lorraine and small portions of Belgium were simply absorbed into the Reich. As might be expected, their conquest and annexation were heavily commemorated through the medium of postal propaganda.

In this example from Lorraine (opposite top), one sees "Lothringen" overprinted stamps as well as postmarks bearing the names of a town renamed in German. In this particular case, the town's name change was subtle. Careful inspection reveals that the German "Sankt" replaced the French "Saint" in the town of St. Martinsbann. The Alsace and Lorraine overprints were valid until the end of 1941 but were then supplanted by regular German issues. Likewise, similar overprints were used in Luxembourg until later being replaced with regular German issues.

A massive propaganda campaign was also conducted regarding the return to Germany of the tiny region around the Belgian towns of Eupen and Malmedy. These towns and their accompanying territories belonged to Germany prior to World War One and were given to Belgium under the terms of the Versailles Treaty. World War Two gave Germany the opportunity to retake this area as well. A set of special commemorative stamps was available throughout Germany to celebrate this historic return of territory. The example here (opposite bottom) bears a special Eupen May 18, 1940 postmark with the propaganda message: "Homecoming to the Greater German Fatherland." A similar postmark was used in the town of Malmedy as well. However it would be lost on American soldiers in the Battle of the Bulge over four years later that the territory on which they fought was considered by Germans to be an integral part of German territory and not merely "occupied Belgium."

Envelope postmarked in occupied Lorraine. German postal authority. *Author's Collection.*

Stamps commemorating the German annexation of Eupen and Malmedy, postmarked in Eupen. German postal authority. *Author's Collection.*

The German invasion of the Soviet Union in 1941 required the total mobilization of the German nation. Once again, great thought was put into the establishment and maintenance of the postal system in the occupied areas as well as the military "feldpost" for the fighting men. The Soviet Union was organized into two primary postal areas initially. Germany dubbed Belarus and the Baltic States as "Ostland," and the vast Ukraine would receive its own unique postal designation. Shown below are examples of postage stamps for these areas that were regular German stamps overprinted with "Ostland" or "Ukraine." While regular German postage stamps were also valid, the so-called "Hitler head overprints" were the stamps most commonly used.

One is struck by the intense propaganda efforts on the part of the authorities to make those territories that were actually incorporated into the Reich proper to appear to be an "ordinary" part of Germany. As pointed out previously, cities with Polish, Czech or French names were renamed in German. If they had been part of pre-World War One Germany or Austria, they reverted to their previously used names. If never a part of Germany, these cities sometimes received new names altogether. In either case, it was unacceptable for an actual portion of the German Reich to bear a Slavic or otherwise foreign name. The map shown opposite indicates the vast scale of territories that Germany actually incorporated into the Reich.[5]

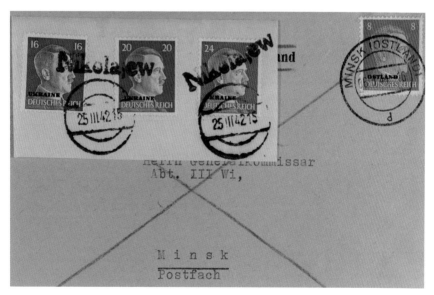

Postage stamps from Ukraine and Ostland (occupied Soviet Union). German postal authority. *Author's Collection.*

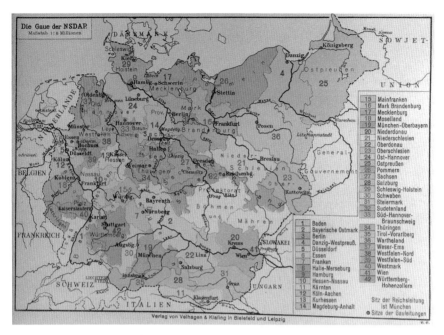

Map of "Greater Germany" in 1941. Map #16 of Europe, reprinted from *Volksatlas*. Published by Velhagen and Klasings. *Atlas is from author's own collection.*

As the map reveals, Hitler went far beyond merely restoring lands lost in World War One. For example, in what was formerly Poland, the new German border extended almost all the way to the city of Warsaw. The provinces of East Prussia and Wartheland were drawn to include territories which historically had never before been part of either Germany or Austria. In addition, Luxembourg was now part of the province or "gau" of Moselland. Yet, perhaps the most revealing aspect of this map, is that it exposes the intent of this stage of German postal propaganda. Hitler skillfully used the post as a means to keep Germans informed on the expanding borders of their country. Through this continuous postal update technique, he attempted to make such absurd "reclaiming" of territory appear justifiable and natural.

The next postcard well illustrates this propaganda technique (page 110, top). Here, one sees that the Polish city of Plock had become the new German city of "Schroettersburg." Propaganda promoting the "normalcy" of this annexation is revealed by its inclusion in the familiar "Get to Know Germany" series of official postal cards. "Schroettersburg" was described as "Southeast Prussia's largest city, high above the beautiful Weichsel." An earlier card, however, shown here still

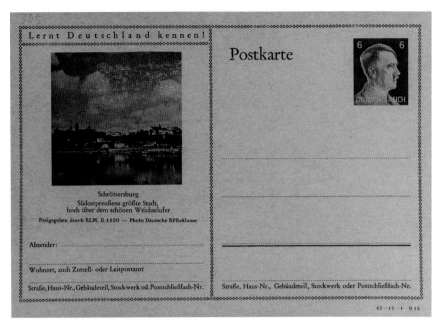

Postcard with photograph of Schroettersburg (the former Plock, Poland) from the "Get to Know Germany" series, 1942. German postal authority. *Author's Collection.*

Postcard with scene of Plock, Poland, before the city was renamed, 1940. German postal authority. *Author's Collection.*

identifies it as "Plock" (opposite below). Presumably, this card predates the renaming of the city by the Germans. However, it is still identified as a part of "Southeast Prussia."

A similar card from the Polish city of Lodz is shown here. Lodz was renamed "Litzmannstadt" and was home to the notorious Jewish ghetto. The message describes this town as follows: "Home of the great textile industry of the German East, entirely the work of German settlement, work and culture." This card, issued in 1941, also contains Nazi inspired racist propaganda. For example, it is implied that Lodz was a productive place only because of *German* influence.

Examples such as these were significant pieces of propaganda for a number of reasons. First, as previously mentioned, they sought to "normalize" the German annexation of new territory. The use of the nearly twenty year old "Get to Know Germany" postcard format put these annexed towns and regions on par with places like Berlin or Hamburg in the minds of the viewer. Second, they served as tangible evidence of Germany's successes on the battlefield. The viewer could see visual evidence of Hitler's territorial triumphs. Furthermore, they presented images of attractive and prosperous structures and places that helped to convince the viewer

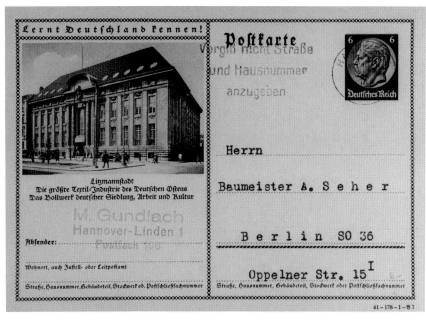

Postcard with scene of Litzmannstadt (the former Lodz, Poland). German postal authority. *Author's Collection.*

either that German influence was already having positive effects or that these already attractive places were therefore worthy of German annexation.

However, in the German racial world view, such postal items were most likely designed to show the pre-existing German nature of these places as indicated by the message found on the Litzmannstadt card. In this context, the German conquest was not a conquest at all, but merely a recognition of the inherent "Germanness" of places crying out for their liberation from Slavic or foreign control. Many such places already had a substantial ethnic German population. Those that did not, would be opened to "colonization" under Germany's plans for the settlement of Germans into such places and the resettlement (or elimination) of Poles and Jews out of such areas.

Finally, postal propaganda of this type also served to put non-German locals on notice of the "new reality." This helped to make what at first might have seemed to have been an absurdity, appear as a serious and irreversible matter to opponents of Germany. As the war finally came to an end, the Allies on both the Eastern and Western fronts seemed shocked at the stubbornness of the German defense of such territories. Obviously, for many, if not most Germans, these regions were not merely occupied; they were thought of as inseparable parts of the territory of Germany.

CHAPTER NINE

The German Feldpost During World War Two

As was seen in World War One, Germany succeeded in providing its troops with an efficient and dependable mail service that continued almost to the very end of the war. As in World War One, this service was entirely free and served as a tremendous source of hope and inspiration for the soldier at the front. On page 114, one sees a feldpost envelope and its contents. The soldier enclosed two photographs with his letter. The bottom photo contains a handwritten message on the back identifying it as a scene in Minsk. The next photo shows a group of soldiers at the side of a railroad car (page 115). The back of this second photo is marked "Minsk-Gomel." It is interesting to note that the railroad scene shows one man on the left side with a faded "x" marked above his head. This was probably the author of this feldpost. The first photo also displays a faded "x" in the snow next to the large building. The significance of this mark is purely guesswork. Perhaps it denotes the location where a soldier friend fell in battle.

In addition to the envelope and photos, is the actual letter written by this soldier (page 116). Several interesting things can be discerned from these items. First, the date that the letter was written was July 3, 1942, and the postmark on the front of the envelope was July 4, 1942. This, in itself, points to the efficiency of the feldpost. The evidence also indicates that the photograph of Minsk covered in snow must have been taken in the winter of 1941-42. Another piece of information one can glean centers around the number "18" found in the letter's upper right corner.

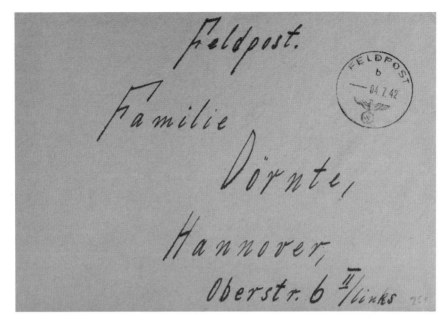

Feldpost envelope, 1942. Private correspondence. *Author's Collection.*

Privately prepared photograph of military quarters in Minsk, 1942. (No information about photographer appears on photograph.) *Author's Collection.*

Privately produced photograph of German troop posing beside train between the cities of Minsk and Gomel. (No information about photographer appears on photograph.) *Author's Collection.*

Soldiers numbered the letters they sent home. That way, if a letter arrived out of sequence, the recipient would know that there were other letters yet to come. This could often happen when a soldier was in transit and letters were handled by two or more different postal regions. A final item worthy of noting is the "42791" found on the upper left corner of the letter. This designated the "feldpost number" of the particular military unit to which the soldier was assigned. Similar to a modern zip code, this number helped insure that the correct unit received the letter even if the unit was reassigned to another area. It also allowed a sender to address a letter without having to know the present location of the soldier in question.

According to Fritz, in his book *Frontsoldaten*, during the course of World War Two, forty to fifty *billion* pieces of German mail were delivered to and from the front with as many as 500 million in a single month.[1] In order to handle this enormous volume, "tens of thousands of people were involved in moving the Feldpost."[2] These statistics seem remarkable when coupled with a realization of the truly vast area of the German fronts during the war. This postal territory included lands north of the Arctic Circle to the Caucasus, all of Western Europe, all of North Africa, as well as thousands of ships and submarines at sea.

One gains a real appreciation for the work involved in merely delivering mail to and from the German soldiers and sailors. This appreciation deepens with the

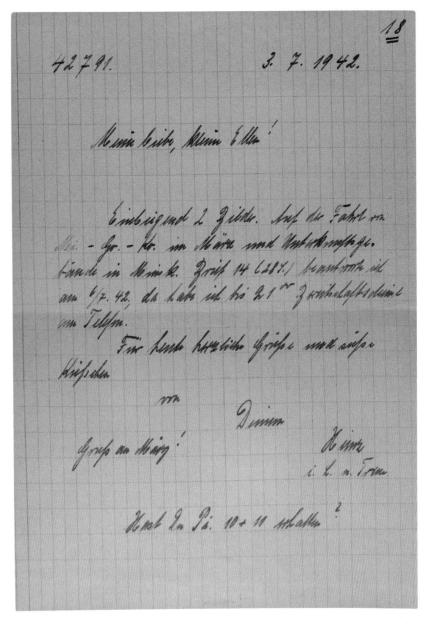

Feldpost letter written by German soldier. (Letter reads: My Dear Little Ellen – Enclosed are two pictures. On the journey from Neidenburg, Ostpreussen, in March, and the quarters in Minsk. I will answer letter 14 on July 6, because I will have stand-by duty at the telephone until July 21. For today, heartfelt greetings and sweet kisses. From your Heinz in love and faith. Greetings to Marg – Have you received letters 10 and 11?) Private correspondence. *Translation courtesy of Dr. Frank Lojewski. Author's Collection.*

knowledge that this mail transit was often done under fire and in the most adverse of conditions. Today, many postal collectors research the various feldpost numbers they find in their collection to try to determine the situation of a particular soldier at the time his letter was mailed.

Having examined a "typical" feldpost letter received in Germany from a soldier at the front, it is important to note that there were also a number of situations in which official mail or soldiers' mail carried more unusual markings or stamps. Special stamps were created for troops stationed in the Adriatic, the islands of the Mediterranean, various local parts of the Soviet Union, North Africa and others. Normally, one would think that the issuance of stamps would be the last thing on the minds of such military units!

For example, someone even took the time to create special stamps and postcards for pockets of German resistance in the Latvian area of Kurland. Two examples of the Kurland stamps are shown below. Kurland represented one of Hitler's most questionable military decisions. While Soviet troops made their way to the West, a

Postage stamps from German enclave of Kurland (Latvia). German postal authority. *Author's Collection.*

couple of hundred thousand German troops held on to an enclave in the Latvian peninsula of Courland (Kurland in German). Late in 1944 and early in 1945, these troops could easily have been evacuated back to the west by sea and might have been useful in slowing the Soviet advance. Instead, Hitler issued one of his notorious orders to hold the area as a "fortress," and these troops held this worthless military position until the end of the war.

From a propaganda perspective, one can discern a threefold benefit of "feldpost" for the Nazi cause. First, the soldiers' morale was greatly boosted through the writing and receiving of mail. This fact is supported in the words of soldier, Harry Mielert, in January 1943. He described the importance of mail in his life: "Days in which no mail comes are not days at all. A few lines can throw a rosy, invigorating light in this desolate realm."[3]

A second propaganda byproduct of feldpost could be seen in the fact that with this mail, Germans back home were kept connected to the front in a tangible way. Family members of soldiers were able to read first hand accounts of the "progress" of the troops. These soldiers' messages must surely have created a heightened sense of support for the Nazi cause as family members struggled to justify the terrors of war.

Finally, the overall message of German efficiency in even being able to provide such a service to soldiers was in itself a sort of propaganda. Surely, those living in Germany during World War Two must have been astonished with this aspect of the power and capabilities of the Nazis. Just as today, one must marvel at the ability of a letter to find its way to a specific soldier in a particular unit who was constantly on the move along Germany's vast front lines.

CHAPTER TEN

The Postal Issues of German Allies and Occupied Territories

A s a part of Germany's occupation policies in Europe, numerous military units were created using volunteer recruits. These existed in Holland, Belgium, France, Scandinavia, Croatia and even Russia. In gratitude for Germany's help in the Civil War, Franco even sent a contingent of Spanish troops. All of these units were sent to the Eastern Front and usually fought under SS auspices as members of the Waffen-SS.[1]

Special postage stamps were often created to commemorate these units. These stamps were valid for postage but often included a surcharge that was purportedly used to assist these local volunteers. It is not clear whether such issues were created at the initiative of officials native to the occupied countries or at Germany's initiative. The propaganda point, however, was to create the impression of a vast European crusade against Bolshevik Russia led by Germany and enthusiastically joined by other Europeans.

Some examples of these types of postal propaganda are shown here. The first (top of page 120) is a feldpost cover bearing stamps printed for the "Legion of French Volunteers Against Bolshevism." These were special airmail stamps created for the use of the Legion. Note that both stamps carry a design featuring an airplane flying over Europe between France and Russia.

During the occupation, France also issued a similar group of postage stamps. The "Tricolor Legion" was featured on a set of two stamps with a surcharge that

Envelope with postage stamps for French troops on Eastern Front. French postal authority. *Author's Collection.*

French postage stamp for the Tricolor Legion. French postal authority. *Author's Collection.*

aided the Legion. Here is one stamp from this set (opposite below). The design featured a legionnaire of the 1940s looking on as Napoleonic forces of the past march ahead. When one considers that these two units of French volunteers, along with a large number of conscripted Frenchmen, had to fight with Germany as citizens of "Greater German" Alsace and Lorraine, an *enormous* number of Frenchmen fought with Germany during World War Two! Undoubtedly, the welcome these soldiers received back home after the war was cold at best.

In Belgium, Hitler characteristically pitted different linguistic groups against one another. There, two "legions" were created. These were the Flanders Legion and the Walloon Legion.[2] In both cases, the stamps created were only for use by the troops. Stamps of these two Belgian legions are shown below and on the next page.

Similar stamps were created in both Norway and the Netherlands (page 123). These issues commemorating their respective "legions" were valid for postage within each country and carried surcharges that benefited the "volunteers" at the front. The stamp at top features a chilling war image from Norway. The bottom illustration shows a Legion souvenir sheet from the Netherlands.

While there are too many other examples to discuss here (including some issues by volunteers from the "Baltic States" and Russia), it is important to make

Postage stamp on postcard to benefit the Flanders legion on Eastern Front. Belgian postal authority. *Author's Collection.*

Postage stamp on postcard to benefit the Walloon legion on Eastern Front. Belgian postal authority. *Author's Collection.*

some mention of Croatia. When Germany invaded Yugoslavia in 1941, a state of Croatia was created which was to be governed by the extreme right wing Ustashi party. The exile, Ante Pavelic, was brought back to Croatia and governed from Zagreb as dictator in a government that was closely allied with its German sponsors. Croatia sent many men to fight on the Eastern Front and even issued numerous stamps and souvenir sheets commemorating the exploits of Croatian soldiers. Many of the Croatian stamp issues portrayed a more fierce and ruthless image than similar issues of other nations.

The first sheet portraying the Croatian Legion (seen on page 124) includes the only stamp issued by an Axis nation to commemorate the loss at Stalingrad. The second stamp (shown on page 125) was part of a set commemorating the elite "Black Legion." It portrays fierce hand-to-hand combat and includes the emblem of the Ustashi Party in the upper left corner. By some accounts, Croatian soldiers were said to be among the most reliable of German allies on the Eastern Front during the war. Very few ever returned home because of the relative large numbers who, quite literally, fought to the death. This reputation also led to the placement of these soldiers in more dangerous situations further contributing to the high

Right: Norweigian postage stamp commemorating the Norway legion. Norwegian postal authority. *Author's Collection.*

Below: Netherland postage stamps commemorating the Netherlands legion. Netherlands postal authority. *Author's Collection.*

ZEGEL, UITGEGEVEN TEN BATE VAN HET VOORZIENINGSFONDS VAN HET NEDERLANDSCH LEGIOEN. 1942.

Croatian stamp sheet commemorating the Croatian legion. Croatian postal authority. *Author's Collection.*

mortality rate. Furthermore, many historians believe that the Croatian Ustashi regime may have even rivaled that of the Nazis' for shear blood thirstiness.[3]

The examples discussed in this chapter represent just a few of the postal materials that were produced by countries either allied with or occupied by Germany during this time period. Other examples could be sited from countries such as Slovakia, Serbia, Albania, and other regions that found themselves under German control. All in all, the German allies and occupied areas printed a vast amount of postal material during World War Two. These materials were one more tool that Hitler used in his propaganda campaign to convince the masses (and perhaps even himself) that his agenda enjoyed great support both inside and outside of Germany.

Croatian postage stamp depicting the Black Legion. Croatian postal authority. *Author's Collection.*

CHAPTER ELEVEN

Postal Materials in the Aftermath

This study of World War Two postal propaganda could not be closed properly without taking a moment to reflect upon the aftermath of World War Two and its manifestation in postal materials. This war left Germany and most of Europe in ruins. Millions of men, women and children were dead. Following the end of the war, the horrifying results of Germany's "final solution" against the Jews was finally made evident to the world. Those men not killed in battle often remained in captivity for many years after the end of the war. This was especially true of those who had the misfortune to find themselves in Russian captivity.

One of the most moving (and chilling) examples of the war's harsh aftermath is graphically illustrated by the postcard seen opposite. It is a 1947 postcard mailed after the war by a German prisoner of war to his son on his son's 8th birthday. The card was lovingly handmade with colored pencils using the reverse side of a standard "Red Cross/Red Crescent" postcard commonly used by prisoners of war. The postcard is dated November 1947 and bears a moving message: "My Dear Child: On your 8th birthday, heartfelt greetings, many thousands of kisses, all the best wishes as well for success at school. If you are very good, perhaps I will be home soon. Good bye, Your Papa." At the bottom he adds: "Greetings and Kisses to Mommy." Two and a half years after the end of the war this man remained in Russian captivity!

Few Germans survived Russian captivity. One can only speculate as to how old his son might have been when this father last saw him and if they ever saw one

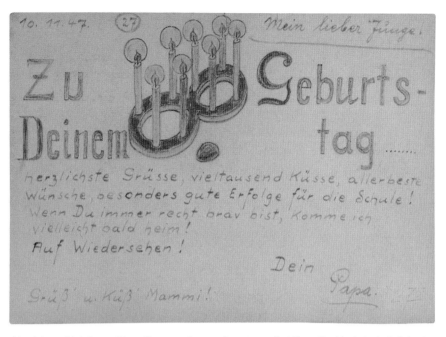

Hand drawn birthday card from German prisoner of war to son. Red Cross Card back. *Author's Collection.*

Address side of prisoner of war card to son. Red Cross Card front. *Author's Collection.*

another again. The front side of the card indicates that the son and mother were in Nuremberg at this time. If that was where they had always lived, then perhaps their own particular wartime experiences were not greatly different from those of most Germans. However, Nuremberg and other cities in the German West became home to millions of men, women and children who were driven from the German East in the first years after the war. The wartime experiences of these eastern refugees were often nearly unbearable.[1]

Another symbolic representation of the aftermath of the war can be seen in the postal item shown below from Breslau. The Silesian city of Breslau had a population of over 615,000 in 1939 and was one of the most significant cities of the German East.[2] This postcard dates from the 1930s and shows Breslau as a thriving metropolis. One sees people walking about past the well-kept shops and a very "modern" building on the right side of the card.

The next photo documents the "new" Breslau after the war. This city was the site of one of the most fanatical of Germany's "last stands" of the war. After the war, Breslau became the Polish city of Wroclaw. Not only did the entire language, culture and character of this city change from German to Polish, but its German citizens were driven out entirely. Most of these people immigrated into what remained of Germany. In 1946, the renowned photographer, John Vachon, was

Photo postcard of prewar Breslau street scene. Published by Kunstverlag, Bruno Scholz, Breslau. *Author's Collection.*

128

Photograph of German refugees fleeing Breslau after the war. Photograph by John Vachon. *Reprinted by permission of Ann Vachon.*

sent into Poland by the United Nations to document the conditions there. In 1995, his photographs and letters from this trip were published in a book entitled, *Poland 1946.* Here is one of Vachon's photographs (above) featuring the same "modern" building seen on the previous postcard. Already, the sign on the building was changed to Polish. The caption reads simply, "German Deportees, Wroclaw." This intersection of the once bustling city of 615,000 was now the scene of some of the last, pathetic German refugees hauling their few belongings out of the city with the help of handcarts.

Hitler's "Greater Germany" whose borders briefly extended all the way to Warsaw in the east, Italy in the South and included Alsace, Lorraine, Luxembourg and Northern Schleswig was now gone. In its place was a "rump Germany" divided between four hostile powers. Cities and regions which had been unquestionably "German" in character and geography for over a thousand years were now lost to Germany forever. Much of what did remain inside the new borders of the nation was in ruins.

Little could illustrate this new face of Germany better than this next set of three postcards created after the war (pages 130-132). These cards were printed in

Postal artcard with scenes of Leipzig Square, Berlin, 1933 and 1945. Published by Berlin-Neuroder Kunstanstalten, Berlin. *Author's Collection.*

Postal artcard with scenes of Berlin Cathedral, Berlin, 1933 and 1945. Published by Berlin-Neuroder Kunstanstalten, Berlin. *Author's Collection.*

Postal artcard with scenes of Reichstag building, Berlin, 1933 and 1945. Published by Berlin-Neuroder Kunstanstalten, Berlin. *Author's Collection.*

English and were designed to be sent home by American and British soldiers. The postcards feature before (1933) and after (1945) scenes of Berlin. These three views, sum up the ultimate fate of Nazi Germany in a manner that truly brings to life the devastating results of Nazism and German militarism. The top scene on the first card depicts Leipzig Square in 1933 filled with traffic and streetcars with a backdrop of beautiful buildings. The 1945-46 scene at the bottom of this card shows the same street with piles of rubble where the buildings once stood with the traffic now reduced to a small handful of pedestrians with carts or bicycles. Similarly, the second card shows a beautiful Berlin Cathedral contrasted with a ruined heap below. Even the heads of statues were blown off in the fighting. The final card shows the grand Reichstag building in 1933 surrounded by stately trees. This image is contrasted with the war blasted Reichstag building surrounded by fallen trees in 1945- 46.

With these postcards one comes full circle in this study of the postal propaganda of the Third Reich. One recalls the young Germany which pioneered the art of postal cards and reveled in the creation and collection of stamps and postal material. This same Germany, in 1946, finds that the very same medium that hailed her "triumphs" now bears witness to her total destruction and the radical dismemberment of her lands. Her postcards once served as the vehicle for proclaiming a message of racial hatred and national strength and chronicled the enlargement of the nation and the conquest of her enemies. Now, her postcards documented the tragedy of war and were merely a means for "starving artists" to make a small sum of money from the sale of their work to foreign occupiers. Gone are the messages of strength, efficiency and hatred. In their place are the messages of devastation, pathos and death as vast segments of the German population in 1946 were now either dead, missing or in enemy captivity. Yet, these bleak images only dimly reflect the total devastation and suffering to be endured by "survivors" of the war. "The postwar turmoil of hand-to-mouth survival many Germans say was starker than the war."[3]

Conclusion

The study of the Third Reich is one that fascinates many researchers and readers alike. Over the years, students of history have been literally inundated with thousands upon thousands of books on the subject. Scholars have examined the rise to power, the personalities of the Reich, the Holocaust, the war and hundreds of other topics. The subject has even captured the imaginations of numerous fiction writers.

The topic of propaganda in the Third Reich has been examined as well. Great research has been done of Hitler's propaganda apparatus, led by Joseph Goebbels. Scholars recognize that propaganda was instrumental in allowing the Third Reich to come into power and to eventually control nearly every aspect of daily life for both German citizens and soldiers:

> When every contemporary book people read, every newspaper, every film they see, every broadcast they hear for years on end is permeated with the same spirit, the same propaganda, they are no longer able to relate what they see and hear to alternative reports; they lose their judgment . . . . the same principles of propaganda. . . held good for postage stamps. The stamp reaches an even larger public.[1]

Therefore, it is curious that so little attention has been paid to the use of stamps and postal material as a form of Nazi German propaganda. It is hard to imagine any other form of official propaganda with the potential to reach as many people. For postal materials had the ability to penetrate the homes of virtually each and every German and the units of each and every soldier. The people had such broad and consistent exposure to this form of propaganda that its messages could be absorbed almost subconsciously. This ability to disarm the masses in such an innocent manner made this type of material particularly effective, powerful, and even "poisonous."

While Germany may have been late in discovering the potential of postal materials as propaganda, as compared to other nations, she nonetheless had the resources at her disposal to make the most of this medium. Germany's reputation as a pioneer in printing and in the production of postal cards combined with her tradition of fierce nationalism. These factors made it much easier for Hitler and the Nazi regime to use this form of propaganda to their greatest advantage.

While the young NSDAP was producing and distributing postal cards as early as 1923, the medium did not really come into its own until 1933, when Hitler was appointed Chancellor. From that point forward, the postal medium became an active and effective participant in the German propaganda infrastructure. Stamps, postcards and even postmarks were able to convey the exact messages that the regime thought the German people needed to see. They were used to show Germans and the world the results of the Reichstag fire, to urge a "yes" vote on a national referendum and to instill an almost religious reverence for Hitler. Indeed, postal propaganda was a vitally important, effective, and efficient means of getting out these official messages to the masses. Yet this form of propaganda has commonly been overlooked in previous studies.

Sometimes, as in the case of the Sudeten annexation, the postal material of the day even gives a glimpse of how individual communities responded enthusiastically to what those in the West might interpret strictly as German aggression. Similarly, ordinary Germans seemed quite willing to purchase postcards and stamps with particularly patriotic or militaristic portrayals. They often even signed them with the words "Heil Hitler" to further prove the widespread public support for Hitler and his government.

Furthermore, the use of such material both before and during the war illustrates how stamps, postcards and special cancellations were used to inspire public support for the war, the regime's murderous tactics and the Nazi's racist hatred. Postal materials were a handy tool for the war's propaganda. They were used for the photographic and artistic glorification of the military, the portrayal of living conditions within the Soviet Union, the dissemination of contempt for the Jews and the continuous updating on new territorial expansion. Unknowingly, every German could, and did, play an active role in perpetuating this aspect of Hitler's propaganda scheme each time they purchased a stamp, mailed a postcard, or retrieved an item from the mailbox.

Finally, it is ironic to note how this very same medium of communications drove home to every German, as well as millions around the world, what price had to be paid for the nation's crimes after the war. Whether it was a hand made birthday card from a German POW to his young son or a picture postcard portraying once grand Berlin buildings now in ruins, this method of communication still played an important role. In the years immediately after the war, the German mailboxes once filled with the "glories" of Hitler and Nazism, now house images of the death, captivity and destruction which were the only lasting results of the Reich's once "glorious" dreams.

There remains much research that can be done in this area of study. While historians have explored a myriad of issues related to the Third Reich, the lack of information regarding postal materials and their impact leaves room for additional investigation. It would be interesting to research sales numbers for German postage stamps of the time. This data could be used to help answer a number of interesting questions. For example, did German consumers buy fewer or more stamps and postal cards with the most blatant Nazi images on them? If given a choice, were Germans more likely to purchase a postcard with a picture of a landscape or a picture of Hitler? Other research could be done to determine what legal sanctions, if any, existed for those who mutilated or inverted the image of Hitler on a postage stamp. Perhaps most importantly, studies could be conducted to determine what impact these postal propaganda images had on the people who saw so many thousands of them during the period from 1933-1945.

Hopefully, other scholars will delve deeper to find answers to some of these fascinating questions. For it is certain that the images and messages seen by Germans on their stamps, postcards and postmarks did have had an incredible impact on shaping public perceptions. While other forms of propaganda, such as posters or films, have received more attention from historians, postal materials should also be acknowledged as one of the most significant forms of propaganda in the Third Reich. Their sheer volume alone undoubtedly made them as important as almost any other medium.

The propaganda messages and images found on each Nazi German stamp and postcard, could be compared to a single drop of venom. By itself, no one item could have wielded much influence in the shaping of public opinion. But when all of these images, or drops of poison, were combined over and over again for many years, they definitely became a powerful and lethal tool of the Third Reich and influenced the minds of millions.

Notes

Notes to Introduction

1. Milton Mayer, *They Thought They Were Free: The Germans 1933-45,* (Chicago: University of Chicago Press, 1966), 51.

2. Anthony Rhodes, *Propaganda, The Art of Persuasion: World War II,* (New York: Chelsea House, 1976), dust jacket.

Notes to Chapter One

1. Otto Hornung, *Illustrated Encyclopedia of Stamp Collecting,* (New York: Hamlyn, 1970), 15.

2. Ibid, 36.

3. Ibid, 48.

4. Ibid, 11-50.

5. W. Raife Wellsted and Stuart Rossiter, *The Stamp Atlas,* (New York: Facts on File Publications, 1986), 62-72.

6. Klaus P. Fischer, *Nazi Germany: A New History,* (New York: Continuum, 1995), 315-316.

7. James K. Pollock, *The Government of Greater Germany,* (New York: D. Van Nostrand Company, 1940), 8.

8. Hornung, *Illustrated Encyclopedia of Stamp Collecting,* 54.

9. Ibid, 55.

10. H. W. Koch, *A History of Prussia,* 2d ed., (New York: Dorset Press, 1987), 78.

11. Edwin Dreschel, *Norddeutscher Lloyd Bremen: 1857-1970; History-Fleet-Ship Mails,* vol. 1, (Vancouver: Cordillera, 1994), 406

Notes to Chapter Three

1. Alan Bullock, *Hitler: A Study in Tyranny,* abr. ed., (New York: Harper Perennial, 1971), 78.
2. Ibid.
3. Anthony Rhodes, *Propaganda, The Art of Persuasion: World War II,* (New York: Chelsea House, 1976), 11.
4. Richard Bessel, *Life in the Third Reich,* (Oxford: Oxford UP, 1987), 305.
5. H. W. Koch, *A History of Prussia,* 2d ed., (New York: Dorset Press, 1987), 305.
6. Ibid, 13.
7. Otto Friedrich, *Before the Deluge: A Portrait of Berlin in the 1920s,* (New York: Harper & Row, 1972), 126.
8. Ibid, 127.
9. Ibid, 128.

Notes to Chapter Four

1. Adolf Hitler, *Mein Kampf,* trans. Ralph Manheim, (Boston: Houghton Mifflin, 1971), 184.
2. Ibid, 176.
3. Milton Mayer, *They Thought They Were Free: The Germans 1933-1945,* (Chicago: University of Chicago Press, 1966), 82.
4. Richard Grunberger, *The 12-Year Reich: A Social History of Nazi Germany 1933-1945,* (New York: Da Capo Publishing, 1995), 82.
5. R. James Bender, *Postcards of Hitler's Germany,* vol. 2, (San Jose: R. James Bender Publishing, 1998), 28.
6. Grunberger, *The 12-Year Reich: A Social History of Nazi Germany, 1933-1945,* 203.
7. Ibid, 203-204.
8. Ibid, 204.
9. Klaus P. Fischer, *Nazi Germany: A New History,* (New York: Continuum 1995), 375-376.

Notes to Chapter Five

1. David Schoenbaum, *Hitler's Social Revolution: Class and Status in Nazi Germany 1933-1939,* (New York: Norton, 1980), 237.
2. Klaus P. Fischer, *Nazi Germany: A New History,* (New York: Continuum, 1995), 425.
3. R. James Bender, *Postcards of Hitler's Germany,* vol. 2, (San Jose: R. James Bender Publishing, 1998), 237.
4. Johannes Steinhoff, Peter Pechel and Dennis Showalter, *Voices From the Third Reich: An Oral History,* (New York: Da Capo Press, 1994), 107.
5. Continental Cartography Company, *Der Grosse Conti Atlas Fur Kraftfahrer,* 18th ed, (Hannover: Der Continental Caoutchaouc-Compagnie G.M.B.H., [1938]), 34.
6. Richard Bessel, ed., *Life in the Third Reich,* (Oxford: Oxford UP, 1987), 52.

Notes to Chapter Six

1. Richard Grunberger, *The 12-Year Reich: A Social History of Nazi Germany, 1933-1945,* 72.

2. Ibid, 75.

3. Anthony Rhodes, *Propaganda, The Art of Persuasion: World War II,* (New York: Chelsea House, 1976), 12.

4. Grunberger, *The 12-Year Reich: A Social History of Nazi Germany, 1933-1945,* 72.

5. R. James Bender, *Postcards of Hitler's Germany,* vol. 2, (San Jose: R. James Bender Publishing, 1998), 309.

6. Anna Maria Sigmund, *Women of the Third Reich,* (Ontario: NDE Publishing, 2000), 172-173.

7. Grunberger, *The 12-Year Reich: A Social History of Nazi Germany, 1933-1945,* 442.

8. Daniel Jonah Goldhagen, *Hitler's Willing Executioners: Ordinary Germans and the Holocaust,* (New York: Alfred A. Knopf, 1996), 77.

9. David J. Hogan, ed., *The Holocaust Chronicle,* (Lincolnwood, Illinois: Publications International, Ltd., 2001), 118-119.

10. Ibid, 323.

11. Ibid.

12. Stephen G. Fritz, *Frontsoldaten: The German Soldier in World War II,* (Lexington: UP of Kentucky, 1995), 203.

13. Ibid, 205.

14. Avraham Barkai, *From Boycott to Annihilation: The Economic Struggle of German Jews 1933-1943,* William Templer, trans., (Hanover: UP of New England, 1985), 153.

15. Ibid, 161.

16. Ibid, 162.

17. Ibid, 161.

Notes to Chapter Seven

1. Anthony Rhodes, *Propaganda, The Art of Persuasion: World War II,* (New York: Chelsea House, 1976), forward.

2. Johannes Steinhoff, Peter Pechel and Dennis Showalter, *Voices From the Third Reich: An Oral History,* (New York: Da Capo Press, 1994), 21.

3. William Sheridan Allen, *The Nazi Seizure of Power: The Experience of a Single German Town 1930-1935,* (New York: Watts, 1973), 208.

4. Guy Sajer, *The Forgotten Soldier: The Classic WWII Auto-Biography,* (Washington: Brassey's [US], 1990), 218.

5. William P. Yenne, *German War Art: 1939-1945,* (New York: Crescent Books, 1983), 56.

6. Stephen G. Fritz, *Frontsoldaten: The German Soldier in World War II,* (Lexington: UP of Kentucky, 1995), 124.

Notes to Chapter Eight

1. G. Donald Hudson, ed., *Encyclopaedia Brittanica World Atlas,* (Chicago: Encyclopedia Britannica, 1945), index 29.

2. Michael Burleigh, *The Third Reich: A New History,* (New York: Hill and Wang, 2000), 579-581.

3. David J. Hogan, ed., *The Holocaust Chronicle,* (Lincolnwood, Illinois: Publications International, Ltd., 2001), 282.

4. Ibid, 282-283.
5. Wolfgang Preuss, ed., *Belhagen & Klasings Grosser Volksatlas,* (Bielefeld, Germany: Velhagen and Klasings, 1941), map 16.

Notes to Chapter Nine
1. Stephen G. Fritz, *Frontsoldaten: The German Soldier in World War II,* (Lexington: UP of Kentucky, 1995), 9.
2. Marc J. Johnson, *In the East,* (New York: Carlton Press, 1994), introduction.
3. Stephen G. Fritz, *Frontsoldaten: The German Soldier in World War II,* (Lexington: UP of Kentucky, 1995), 83.

Notes to Chapter Ten
1. David J. Hogan, ed., *The Holocaust Chronicle,* (Lincolnwood, Illinois: Publications International, Ltd., 2001), 334.
2. Ibid, 245, 256.
3. Stanley G. Payne, *A History of Fascism 1914-1945,* (Madison: U of Wisconsin Press, 1995), 404-411.

Notes to Chapter Eleven
1. Christopher Duffy, *Red Storm on the Reich,* (New York: Atheneum, 1991), 271-292.
2. G. Donald Hudson, ed., *Encyclopaedia Britannica World Atlas,* (Chicago: Encyclopedia Britannica, 1945), index 29.
3. Alison Owings, *Frauen: German Women Recall the Third Reich,* (New Jersey: Rutgers UP, 1995), 471.

Notes to Summary
1. Anthony Rhodes, *Propaganda, The Art of Persuasion: World War II,* (New York: Chelsea House, 1976), 18.

Bibliography

Allen, William Sheridan. *The Nazi Seizure of Power: The Experience of a Single GermanTown 1930-1935*. Chicago: Quadrangle Books, 1965. New York: Watts, 1973.

Barkai, Avraham. *From Boycott to Annihilation: The Economic Struggle of German Jews 1933-1943*. Trans. William Templer. Hanover: UP of New England, 1985.

Bender, R. James. *Postcards of Hitler's Germany*. 2 Vol. San Jose: R. James Bender Publishing, 1998.

Bessel, Richard, ed. *Life in the Third Reich*. Oxford: Oxford UP, 1987.

Bullock, Alan. *Hitler: A Study in Tyranny*. Abr. ed. New York: Harper Perennial, 1971.

Burleigh, Michael. *The Third Reich: A New History*. New York: Hill and Wang, 2000.

Continental Cartography Company. *Der Grosse Conti Atlas Fur Kraftfahrer*. 18th ed. Hannover: Der Continental Caoutchouc-Compagnie G. M. B. H., [1938].

Drechsel, Edwin. *Norddeutscher Lloyd Bremen: 1857-1970; History-Fleet-Ship Mails*. Vol. 1. Vancouver: Cordillera, 1994.

Duffy, Christopher. *Red Storm on the Reich*. New York: Atheneum, 1991.

Fischer, Klaus P. *Nazi Germany: A New History*. New York: Continuum, 1995.

Friedrich, Otto. *Before the Deluge: A Portrait of Berlin in the 1920s*. New York: Harper & Row, 1972.

Fritz, Stephen G. *Frontsoldaten: The German Soldier in World War II*. Lexington: UP of Kentucky, 1995.

Goldhagen, Daniel Jonah. *Hitler's Willing Executioners: Ordinary Germans and the Holocaust*. New York: Alfred A Knopf, 1996.

Grunberger, Richard. *The 12-Year Reich: A Social History of Nazi Germany 1933-1945*. New York: Da Capo Publishing, 1995.

Hitler, Adolf. *Mein Kampf*. Trans. Ralph Manheim. Boston: Houghton Mifflin, 1971.

Hogan, David J. *The Holocaust Chronicle.* Lincolnwood, Illinois: Publications International, Ltd., 2001.

Holt, Tonie and Valmai. *I'll Be Seeing You: Picture Postcards of World War II.* Derbyshire, Eng.: 1987.

Hornung, Otto. *Illustrated Encyclopedia of Stamp Collecting.* New York: Hamlyn, 1970.

Hudson, G. Donald, ed. *Encyclopaedia Britannica World Atlas.* Chicago: Encyclopedia Britannica, 1945.

Johnson, Marc J. *In the East.* New York: Carlton Press, 1994.

Koch, H. W. *A History of Prussia.* 1987 ed. New York: Dorset Press, 1987.

Mayer, Milton. *They Thought They Were Free: The Germans 1933-45.* 1955. Chicago: U of Chicago P, 1966.

Owings, Alison. *Frauen: German Women Recall the Third Reich.* 1993. New Jersey: Rutgers UP, 1995.

Payne, Stanley G. *A History of Fascism 1914-1945.* Madison: U of Wisconsin Press, 1995.

Pollock, James K. *The Government of Greater Germany.* New York: D. Van Nostrand Company, 1940.

Preuss, Wolfgang, ed. *Velhagen & Klasings Grosser Volksatlas.* Bielefeld, Ger.: Velhagen and Klasings, 1941.

Rhodes, Anthony. *Propaganda, The Art of Persuasion: World War II.* New York: Chelsea House, 1976.

Sajer, Guy. *The Forgotten Soldier: The Classic WWII Auto-Biography.* Washington: Brassey's (US), 1990.

Schoenbaum, David. *Hitler's Social Revolution: Class and Status in Nazi Germany 1933-1939.* New York: Norton, 1980.

Sigmund, Anna Maria. *Women of the Third Reich,* Ontario: NDE Publishing, 2000.

Steinhoff, Johannes, Peter Pechel and Dennis Showalter. *Voices From the Third Reich: An Oral History.* New York: Da Capo Press, 1994.

Vachon, Ann, ed. *Poland, 1946: The Photographs and Letters of John Vachon.* Washington: Smithsonian Institution P, 1995.

Wellsted, W. Raife, and Rossiter, Stuart. *The Stamp Atlas.* New York: Facts on File Publications, 1986.

Yenne, William P., ed. *German War Art: 1939-1945.* New York: Crescent Books, 1983.

The Author

Since early childhood, Albert Moore has been an avid collector of stamps and postal materials. In the course of his education, he developed a fascination with European history. While working on his Master s Degree, he decided to combine these two areas of interest. The result is this book. Here, Al seeks to recognize the unique historical record and perspective that can be gleaned from a close examination of Nazi Germany's postal material. Al earned his Bachelor of Arts from Indiana University and Master of Arts from California State University at Dominguez Hills. He lives in Southeastern Indiana with his wife, Diane, and their children, Wesley and Lisa. He is currently First Vice President with a regional investment firm.